Language Teaching Practicum

Seyyed Ali Kazemi, Ph.D.
Leila Zarei, M.A.

Edited by:
Ali Kazemi, Ph.D.

PREFACE

Language Teaching Practicum has been designed to meet the needs of language teachers at the start of their teaching career, at that stage where they are just about to do-or have just done- an initial teaching course. It has been written for teachers who teach learners of whatever age. It introduces the most effective and proven techniques and strategies in language teaching and classroom management.

The main incentive behind preparing this book was to help those who love to be efficient English teachers but don't know how. To our knowledge, this is the first comprehensive book totally devoted to classified major concepts in language teaching and classroom management in one volume. The book has been directed towards the needs and concerns of the English teachers/teachers to be and university instructors.

This book can be used as a textbook for BA/MA courses like *Teaching Language Skills*, *TTC*, and *Practical Language Teaching/Language Teaching Practicum*.

This book, with clear diction appropriate to the competence of its audience, elaborates on the rudiments of practical ELT in five learner friendly chapters, presenting the most prominent language teaching theories and techniques for teaching English as a foreign or second language. Language Teaching Practicum is a practical book, concentrating on teaching practice rather than on a detailed analysis of learning theory. It aims to reflect a range of current teaching and learning styles.

We would very much welcome the oral and written comments and reflections with open arms. Correspondence concerning this book may be addressed to us at Kazemi.TEFL@Yahoo.com.

Seyyed Ali Kazemi
Leila Zarei

CONTENTS

Chapter Five: Principles and Practices of Classroom Assessment 123

Preliminaries

An Overview of Language Teaching Methods and Approaches

What is a method? In an attempt to define "method", it is a good idea to consider the tripartite used by Anthony (1963) that made a distinction of *Approach, Method* and *Technique*. This distinction was developed and reconstructed by Richards and Rodgers (1982, 1985) as *Approach, Design* and *Procedure*, encompassed within the overall concept of **Method**, which is defined as an umbrella term for the specification and interrelation of theory and practice where **approach** refers to the beliefs and theories about language, language learning, and language teaching that underlie a method, **Design** relates the theories of language and learning to the form and function of teaching materials and activities in the classroom, and **Procedure** concerns the techniques and practices employed in the classroom as consequences of particular approaches and designs (Richards & Rodgers, 1985).

If "Method" contains a particular set of features to be followed almost as the ultimate solution, it can be suggested that we are now in a "Post-Method" era where the emphasis is on the looser concept of "Approach" which starts from some basic principles which are then expanded in the design and development of practice. Accordingly, the model according to Richards and Rodgers (1985) might be reconstructed, without existence of "Method".

Grammar translation method (GTM) was based on the use of lexis and grammar in reading, writing, and translation. It ignored speaking and listening. There was no specific theory for learning. Its main objective was increasing students' knowledge in grammar and vocabulary to explore the literature of the target language. The linguistic materials were chosen from predetermined syllabus with regard to deductive method of grammar teaching. Activities in classroom contained reading, translating, explaining grammatical rules, transforming, and making sentences. Learners were quite passive and teachers were in the center of the class. This method did not conform to the communicative competence of the learners.

Direct method (DM) was based on priority of speaking over writing skill, phonetic training to increase native-like pronunciation, the use of dialogs, and inductive grammar teaching. It was believed that learning enhances when learners do not engage in L1 directly and when L2 is acquired in the same way as L1. There was no place for translation. The main objective of DM was to teach everyday-life language through introducing topical syllabus in hierarchical order of grammar and vocabulary. Activities contained naming objects, reading, comprehension questions and answers, and oral activities. Students were asked to perform grammatical activities both in spoken and written forms. Learners actively participate in real-life interactions. Teachers did not use L1 and they focused on real objects, pictures, and/or drawings in vocabulary teaching. This method suffered from its emphasis on the similarity between L1 and L2 acquisition. It resulted in fluency with no accuracy.

Audiolingual method (ALM) was based on starting the class with a dialog on a tape. It contained the theories that language is primarily speaking not writing, language is a set of habits, do not teach about the language but teach the language, a language is what native speakers say, and languages are different. The theory of learning referred to behaviorism, conditioning, stimuli, responses, reinforcement, and overlearning. The objective was gaining proficiency in all four language skills through sound discrimination, improving auditory memory, developing accuracy and fluency, and emphasizing on the teaching of *listening* and *speaking* before reading and writing. The syllabus was based on gradable structural and lexical items considering contrastive analysis. Activities dealt with mimicry memorization of dialogs, repetition, and pattern drills. Learners did not have creativity in the use of language. Teachers controlled all class activities and avoided errors from happening as much as possible. Textbooks, films, pictures, realia, and tapes were perfect materials for ALM. Learners in ALM could not develop communication ability since learning was based on parrot-like fluency.

Cognitive code learning method (CCM) was based on considering language as a rule-governed phenomenon with a set of finite rules, language is infinitely varied and impossible to teach all linguistic aspects that are needed to know, language operates at deep, transformational rules, and surface structure to convey meaning, language is universal and languages have some common elements, and all humans have the capacity to learn languages. Cognitivists who believed in mentalism supported this method and rejected conditioning theory in learning a new language. This approach focused on understanding the grammatical rules through long-term memory. The objective was mastery over four language skills through conscious knowledge of language rules. Gradable materials were selected to make learners familiar with real-life contexts. Learners internalized the grammatical rules and were encouraged to have real-life-like interactions. Teachers taught deductively and tolerated errors and put them into class discussion to help students get away from that situation. The main materials were textbooks, tapes and visual aids. Activities included reading and listening comprehension, using grammatical rules in written exercises, writing summaries and compositions, and oral practice of new items.

Community language learning method (CLL) was based on considering language as a system of sounds, meanings, and grammatical structures that introduced to learners gradually. It focused on the social role of language through interactional and transactional functions of language. Language was considered as a way of exchanging ideas, emotions, and information. Humanistic psychology supported this method through emphasizing the uniqueness and individuality of learners with regard to their biological system, cognitive development, and personality characteristics. CLL enhanced *whole-person learning* by considering learners' styles of learning and their feelings and attitudes. Teachers acted as counselor to help students to solve their problems. Students needed security, attention, aggression to seek self-expression, retention and reflection to internalize new material, and discrimination of items to communicate purposefully. The main objective was making students autonomous. The teacher adjusted the translation of students' utterances with related level of language proficiency. Oral skills and pronunciation were emphasized. They did not have a textbook but a tape-recorder was used. Students discussed around their favorite topics.

Total physical response method (TPR) focused on grammar, imperative sentences, language chunks, and prefabricated patterns. The theory which supported this method was based on the idea that human beings are equipped with a system which enables learners to acquire any language in an order, listening precedes speaking, comprehension should be before production, verbal and nonverbal performance can engage both right and left hemisphere to increase learning, and language learning should take place in a stress-free environment. New grammatical and vocabulary items were introduced through isolated sentences, not in reading passages or dialogs. Learners were mere listeners since speaking was delayed. They gradually produced utterances. Teachers actively provided learners with commands to acquire new grammatical and vocabulary items. Major errors were corrected and minor ones were postponed to more advanced stages. There was no textbook available at early stages and kits were used to expand language learning. Imperative drills, role plays, games, and watching films were used as main activities in TPR. This method was not appropriate for intermediate or advanced adult learners.

Natural approach/method (NA) emphasized that learning (conscious process taking place in class) and acquisition (unconscious process happening in naturalistic settings) are different, linguistic skills should be learned in a predictable and natural order, acquired knowledge is used to communicate and learned knowledge is used to repair the output, learners should be exposed to $i + 1$ which shows that learners need new information one step beyond his/her current stage of linguistic competence, and affective and emotional factors can act as filters. Its objective was enabling adult learners to talk about their ideas and problems. It was a situational and topical approach which introduced basic everyday situations through oral and written communication skills. Learners progressed gradually in order to be capable of communicating successfully. The sources of comprehensible input were teachers who created friendly atmosphere through appropriate selection of materials and activities. Authentic materials from magazines, newspapers, ads, film, etc. were available. Commands, mimes, games, role plays, and group discussion were typical NA activities.

Silent way method (SW) was based on structuralism school of thought presenting language as a set of sounds arbitrarily associated with meanings which are organized through grammatical rules. Linguistic items were taught separately without considering social context through charts and rods. It considered discovery learning, creativity, and problem solving. It was believed that L1 and L2 acquisition are different so that L2 acquisition starts from the known knowledge to the unknown knowledge. Using a pointer and colored charts facilitated the learning process. Learning happened through silent awareness of the task. The focus was on vocabulary, basic grammatical points, pronunciation, and supersegmental rules. Receptive skills received more emphasis than speaking and writing at early stages. Learners were responsible for their own learning. They needed to have high concentration since the teacher did not repeat anything twice. The teachers were unique and used non-verbal cues and gestures. They avoided any interference in the learning process. Errors were elicited from students. Teachers used textbooks, tapes, and visual aids to make variety in teaching. Activities including modeling, oral and physical responses to the teacher, and correcting each other were common in (SW) classes.

Suggestopedia method (SM) was based on using language as a means of communication with the content of lexicon and grammatical rules. Meaningful texts were presented. Direct translation was used to increase students' comprehension of the text. This method dealt with desuggestion (process of unloading learners' memory banks from blocking memory) and suggestion (process of loading the memory banks with desired memories). The terms *asleep, awake, alert, attentive, and anxious* were familiar terms used in this method. Teachers' authority helped learners to feel like a newborn child encouraged through songs, gymnastic exercises, and experiencing infantalization. Learners were provided with posters, musical background, dim light, and high room decoration to gain knowledge from instruction and classroom environment. Baroque music was played to make pseudo-passivity to make physical relaxation and mental concentration. The objectives were achieving advanced speaking proficiency in a short time, increasing memory power, creating problem solving, and enabling learners to learn large amounts of vocabulary and grammatical points. The syllabus followed a topical pattern, a dialog, and a passage with its translation. The learner' mental state was important. The main teacher' role was providing a secure atmosphere to increase learners' confidence through using maps, posters, furniture, role play costumes, yoga, and lights. Activities contained yoga, role plays, class discussion, games, and songs.

Communicative language teaching method (CLT) proposed the concept of *communicative competence* which opposed Chomsky's linguistic competence. *Communicative competence* consists of *grammatical competence*, (knowledge of sounds, words, and grammar), *strategic competence* (ways to initiate, maintain, and terminate communication), *sociolinguistic competence* (knowledge of different social and cultural issues), and *discourse* (competence to interpret elements of a message). Communicative tasks were applied to involve learners in real life interactions through information gap, choice, and feedback. There is no single set of principles to interpret this method. There are some general points of view. Language learning is facilitated when learners are motivated to engage in interaction and meaningful communication, useful classroom learning tasks and exercises are the best sources of negotiating meaning, expanding language resources, and taking part in meaningful interpersonal exchange, communication is a holistic process based on several language skills, language learning is a process of using language through trial and error, learners learn at different rates and have different needs, effective language learning needs effective use of communication strategies, the role of the teacher is a facilitator, and learners need collaboration and sharing in the community of the classroom. Communicative textbooks, interactive tasks such as watching films, and realia such as magazines, ads, articles, and props are used in this method.

The following principles are reflected in the communicative language teaching methodology (Burns and Richards, 2012):

Diversity: these days English students are characterized by diversity, having different needs, motivation, learning strategies, learning styles, abilities, and cultural background. Teachers should take these different characteristics into account considering that students do not learn in a uniform manner. This point of view has made learners more active in preparing the content and approach of learning, supporting learners, and developing learning strategies.

Autonomy of language learning: learners receive more choices to take control over their learning, the content of learning, learning processes based on group-learning, self-assessment, and learner-centered approaches.

The social nature of learning: learning is a social activity not an individual isolated activity. It depends on interaction with others to create motivation for learning. The key condition for language learning is creating a supportive classroom atmosphere based on principles of group dynamics.

Curricular integration: English is not a stand-alone subject but is connected to other subjects. In curriculum designing, learners' out-of-class interests, text-based learning to develop fluency, and project work should be taken into account.

Thinking skills: language learning should be the best place to improve higher-order, critical, and creative thinking. It means that language learning does not convey learning language for its sake but developing thinking skills in situations beyond the classroom.

Focus on meaning: meaning is considered as an important factor of learning. Task-based and content-based teaching can represent this view to seek for meaning through content and tasks.

Teachers as co-learners: in language teaching, teachers should be engaged in a process of expanding their knowledge and   discovering teaching and learning principles through action research and classroom investigation collaboratively.

Re-imagining the nature of teaching: the nature of teaching has been rethought in linguistics based on cognitive and sociocultural points of view. Teacher cognition contains how teachers ' thoughts and beliefs form their understanding of teaching and their classroom techniques. Teaching is not simply the application of learned skills and knowledge but learners' motivations and reactions to the lesson are affected by teachers. Sociocultural point of view emphasizes learning in specific settings or contexts. The location of language learning is different. It may occur in a classroom or an informal setting which can create different potentials for learning.

New view of language proficiency: traditionally language proficiency was considered as focusing on grammar in language learning and language use. Grammar was in the centre of teaching techniques. The development of communicative methodologies has shifted the role of grammar-based methodologies. New trends in authentic language teaching have contained using more explicit treatment of grammar in a text-based situation, applying test activities and tasks based on communicative language use, introducing activities to raise consciousness, and building opportunities for meaningful and communicative practice of grammar.

CHAPTER ONE

Teaching Language Elements Practically
"Better untaught than ill taught." Anonymous

Introduction

kumaravadivelu (1994) defines a **Post-method Pedagogy** as a new perspective that has abandoned the demand for a better method. The Post-method has led to a new focus on the process of learning and teaching rather than putting much emphasis on methods as the key to successful teaching. He sees *parameters of particularity, practicality, and possibility as the axles of the wheel of the language learning and teaching.* The first concept relates to considering particular group of teachers teaching a particular group of learners based on a thourough understanding of local linguistic, socio-cultural, and political particularities. The second concept encourages teachers to theorize from their practice and practice what they theorize. And the third one emphasizes the importance of socio-political consciousness that the participants bring with them to shape identity formation and social transformation.

In the same direction, Brown (2000) believes that *since every learner is unique, every teacher is unique, every learner-teacher relationship is unique, and every context is unique; there is no need for new methods.* That's known as the requiem for methods.

Eclecticism

Since no method, in its entirety, came to be successful, a trend of eclecticism started to flourish in the 1980s and the early 1990s. The idea was originated by Sweet and Palmer in the early decades of the 20[th]century (see Rivers 1981, p 54). They believed that a good method is an eclectic one which requires the teacher to make use of his/her knowledge of language besides his/her experience in psychology. According to H. Palmer's *multiple line of approach*, an eclectic method picks up every good idea and welcomes future developments. Generally, the communicative needs of the learners are crucial in the selection of an array of techniques from different methods.

Major factors in any educational system

There are four major inter-related factors in any educational system to complete the phenomenon of language teaching and learning. It is believed that if the information delivered through the content is interesting and useful, students acquire the language faster. It's essential for teachers to provide a rich context for students to learn the language and practice it as well. Teachers and learners as other integral parts of any educational system maintain communication in the frame of a particular context and setting to establish the specific content of education.

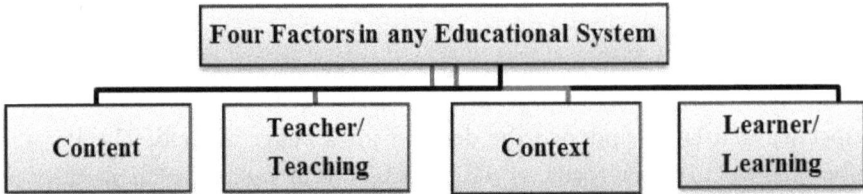

Figure 1.1 *Major Factors in Language Teaching & Learning*

Language elements

In broad terms, language elements are concerned with aspects of **components** and **skills**. Components are subdivided into three different but inter-related areas of grammar, vocabulary and pronunciation. All these three components are manifested in language skills to establish the basis of language system.

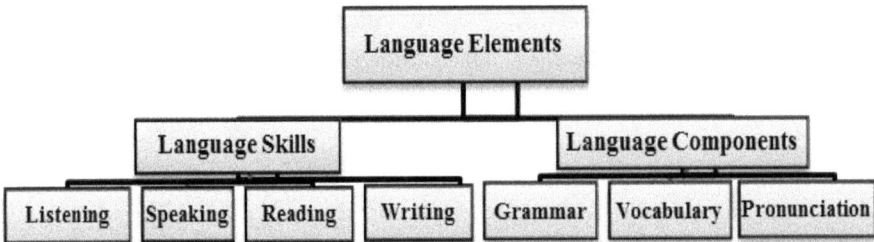

Figure 1.2 *Major Elements in Language Teaching & Learning*

Language skills can be categorized into **written** and **oral** skills. While the two types have some commonalities, they have different subsets.

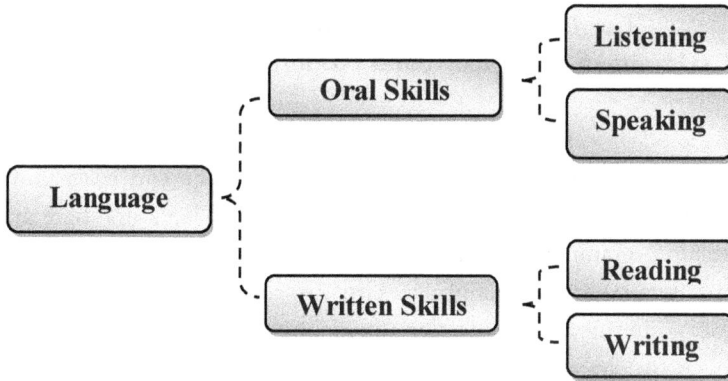

Figure 1.3 *Oral versus Written Skills*

In learning a new language, learners develop both **receptive skills** and **productive skills**. Receptive skills include understanding when learners listen and read. They receive the language and decode the meaning to understand the message. Productive skills are speaking and writing. Learners use the language that they have acquired and produce a message through speech or written text in order to be understood by others.

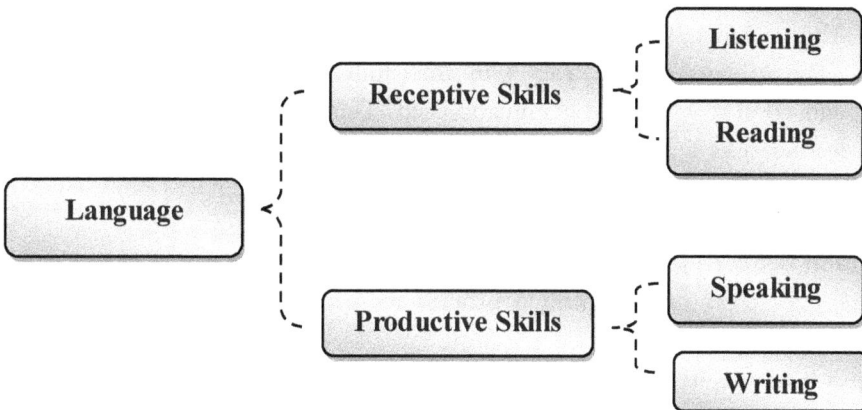

Figure 1.4 *Receptive versus Productive Skills*

Teaching language components
(Grammar, Vocabulary, and Pronunciation)

1. Teaching grammar

The word *Grammar* conjures books full of explanations and rules that may tell how to use verbs, where to use superlatives, etc. That's one part of grammar. Teaching grammar means enabling language students to use linguistic forms accurately, meaningfully, and appropriately. Focusing on grammatical forms during communicative interaction rather than meaning is an obvious way to prevent achieving the goals of teaching English communicatively. It is realistic to regard grammar as an accumulation of different elements, some more systematic than others, some linked together, and some completely independent.

Three-dimensional grammar framework

- **Form / Structure**   How is it formed?
- **Meaning / Semantics**   What does it mean?
- **Use / Pragmatics**   When /why is it used?

The form/structure refers to those lexical and morphological forms to show how a grammar structure is made and how it is arranged in a sentence or text. The meaning/semantics represents the meaning of a grammar structure. The use/pragmatics deals with the study of relations between language and context which are grammaticalized. This part shows when or why the learner uses a special grammar structure instead of another form (Celce-Murcia, 1991).

The relation between grammar and second language learning

There are five stages of the learning process to arrive at a rationale for teaching grammar.

The Input Stage refers to language sources used to initiate learning process. At this stage, teachers should focus on simplification of input through a limited set of tenses and structures, frequency of exposure to bring several possibilities of the structure, explicit/implicit instruction, and raising consciousness to make learners aware of linguistic features in the input.

The Intake Stage is the comprehended input to remain in long term memory. The complexity, importance, frequency, and needs are salient factors to be considered at this stage.

The Acquisition Stage is the process of incorporating a new learning item into learners' developing system. Learners can acquire a new language through **noticing** (recognizing differences between forms of new language and target like forms), **discovering rules** (identifying the underlying grammatical rules for example in word order, and phrasal structure), **reconstructing** (mediating intake into the developing system), and **experimentation** (trying out new language forms).

The Access Stage refers to the learner's ability to use his/her new learning item during communication.

The Output Stage refers to active use of language production coherently and correctly.

An English teacher should be aware of all these stages to foster learning (Richards & Renandya, 2003).

Guidelines for preparing new grammatical structures for teachers

Select the grammatical item you want to teach.

Adjust the selection to consider precisely what is/isn't going to be included.

List situations, places in which the language is usually used.

Prepare some sentences with using the new grammatical item in a natural way.

Choose one of the realistic sentences as a target one.

Decide on a situational context to focus on the language form.

Analyze the form of the target sentence, the regularities, and the nuts and bolts to make a new sentence.

Analyze the meaning by looking at the meaning components of lexical items, the meaning of lexical items in context, and meaning in relation to words.

Check the pronunciation of the target language.

Diagnose students' problems.

Decide what you hope learners could fulfill in a lesson.

PPP Approach (Presentation, Practice, and Production) has had a long history in teaching English as second/foreign language. Like all teaching approaches, despite all advantages, this approach has some disadvantages as well. It is believed that this approach is a product-oriented approach that focuses on controlled manners of using exercises to produce automatic use of language. This view of sequential language learning has been criticized that it does not support the process-oriented approaches of learning language. In spite of all criticisms, this approach is durable and deals with practical and effective procedures for maintaining control of the classroom. This approach, along with communicative approaches suggested in this book, provides learners with an ideal atmosphere to acquire English (Ellis, 2004).

Teaching grammar in practice

1. **Warm-up and awareness-rising:** the teacher can have a warm-up in a variety of ways, such as:

    - Using students' own experience
    - Making use of previously gained knowledge
    - Benefiting from sentences of the book

2. **Presentation:** in this part, the new structure is clarified and students become familiar with its form, and then take the following steps *interactively.*

    - Try to present memorable interesting examples.
    - Avoid unnecessary grammar instruction.
    - Put several examples on the board (preferably students' own examples) and draw students' attention to the form of the examples.
    - Use simple examples and solid colors to make particular effects.
    - Use visual aids such as charts, maps, drawings, and objects to teach tenses and prepositions.
    - Integrate form with meaning in grammar instruction.
    - Avoid grammar and vocabulary mistakes.
    - Use *highlighting and underlining techniques* to increase students' attention.

Types of presentation of grammar

Inductive presentation: using specific facts and examples to form general rules and principles (for both children and adults)

Deductive presentation: using explicit grammar rules from general to specific examples (for adults)

Types of instruction

- **Explicit instruction:** making students aware of language forms consciously
- **Implicit instruction:** teaching language rules without awareness of what has been taught

3. Practice

- For this phase, the students repeat the examples written on the board.
- Next, the teacher has a variety of drills on the structure, including **substitution, transformation**, etc.
- For *pre-intermediate students*, there should be *more drills*, while for *intermediate* and *post-intermediate students, just a few may suffice*.
- **Internalization** and **feedback** are important for teachers.

4. Doing the exercises of the book

- The teacher can divide the students into groups and require them to do the exercises.
- The teacher should act as a *guide* and *facilitator*.

5. Comparing answers

- Students compare their answers in pairs.
- After they have compared their answers, several of them should be selected to read their answers aloud.

6. Production and personalization

- Students are supposed to make sentences based on the new structure.
- The sentences should be based on their personal information.

7. Assignment

- Students should write some sentences using the new structure.
- They can write a short paragraph using the new structure.

Grammar is the by-product of communication i.e., the purpose is communication. Therefore, students should insert the new points to their speech.

Grammar gap in task work

Teaching grammar should be based on task performance not a predetermined grammar syllabus. However, developing acceptable levels of grammatical proficiency through this kind of approach is problematic.

Grammar in task work

In order to focus on form as communicative approach to teaching, the following points can be useful.

- The exposure to language should be based on an appropriate level of difficulty.
- Engagement in meaning-focused interaction in the language should be considered.
- Opportunities should be prepared for learners to notice linguistic forms while involving in language.

Teaching grammar using communicative tasks

What do students say and do? There are some statements about what students sometimes say and do.

- Students often complain that they know all the grammar, but they cannot use it correctly while speaking.
- Students cannot often understand the relevance of learning grammar.
- Students say they need more feedback on the language they produce.
- Students say they like to do more speaking in classes.
- Students can often do very controlled oral practice activities correctly. However, when they are given a freer practice activity, they will often get the target grammar wrong.

Solution

Using communication activities to teach grammar can provide variety for students and cater to the needs of learners who are keen on developing their ability to use English. It also provides opportunities for teachers to give systematic feedback on students' errors.

Communicative tasks

- The teacher writes all collected errors on the board. Corrections can either be elicited from learners, or students can be put in pairs or small groups to correct the language and conduct feedback.
- The teacher gives students another communication activity to practice the target language point and asks them to do this activity and concentrate on using the target grammar point correctly. Alternatively, students could re-do the original activity.

- Having elicited corrections of student language, the teacher uses oral concept questions to monitor the meaning of the target grammar point, afterwards checking the form by eliciting it and then writing it up on the board.
- The teacher monitors and listens carefully to the language that students are producing, especially for the target grammar point, or its absence and finds out what incorrect forms students are using in its place. The teacher also notes other examples of incorrect language, noting these down on a piece of paper.
- The teacher sets up the communication activity, but makes a point of not mentioning the target grammar point nor asking that students use it.

2. Teaching vocabulary

Approaches to vocabulary teaching

In the past, vocabulary teaching and learning received little attention in second or foreign language settings, but recently there has been a great interest in the significance of vocabulary and its importance in learning and teaching. It is a core component of language proficiency and provides much of the foundation for how well learners learn a new language. According to Hunt and Beglar (1998), there are three approaches to vocabulary teaching and learning:

- **Incidental learning** (as a by-product of doing other things through extensive reading)
- **Explicit instruction** (as identifying specific vocabulary targets for learners, knowing approximately 3,000 high-frequency for effective reading, while knowing 5,000 words for academic success)
- **Independent strategy development** (as strategies for inferring words by guessing from context)

Combinations of all three approaches are suggested.

The steps for teaching vocabulary in practice

1. **Write the new word on the board:** the first thing a teacher should do is to put the new word on the board and read it aloud for everyone.
2. **Emphasize on related word injection:** new related vocabulary can be injected.
3. **Help the students to learn how to guess the meaning of new words:** using the context is helpful to guess new expression.
4. **Clarify the meaning of new words (if necessary):** if students are not able to guess the meaning, the teacher should clarify it using synonyms, antonyms, examples, objects, illustrations, gestures, stems, etc.
5. **Practice the word's parts of speech:** the teacher elicits the word's parts of speech (noun, verb, adjective, adverb, preposition…) and writes them on the board in front of the new word. Try to draw students' attention to the grammatical points.
6. **Involve students in repetition and production:** once the activity is over and all the new words have been listed on the board, students should be asked to repeat them and make sentences with the **active** ones.

Important points in teaching vocabulary

- Learners need to learn more than the form. They need to hear pronunciation, recognize syllable structure, and stress pattern.
- Learners should be taken away from learning words with similar forms at the same time. It increases the chance of confusion.
- It is more effective to teach learners over several short sessions than one longer session.
- The students should be asked to study five or seven words at a time.
- The teacher can provide opportunities for incidental learning through extensive reading (in advanced levels).
- The teacher should help students how to use dictionaries.
- The students can be familiar with electronic dictionaries with its multimedia annotations.
- Collocation associations help the learner in maintaining new words in memory.
- It is necessary for students to know "mnemonic device," to link a word form with its meaning in memory.

Practices, activities, and games

- Matching pictures to new vocabularies
- Matching parts of vocabularies to other parts, e.g. beginnings and endings
- Matching vocabularies to others, e.g. collocations, synonyms, opposites
- Using prefixes and suffixes to make new vocabularies
- Filling in crosswords
- Filling in gaps

Vary the way you explain

- Demonstrate convincingly through planned and unplanned vocabulary teaching.
- Use real things or draw sketches to teach concrete objects to beginners and situational pictures cut from magazines and catalogs for intermediate learners.
- Use the board to show scales or grades.
- Apply antonyms/synonyms and roots/affixes to analyze a word into its building blocks.

- Make verbal explanations to introduce abstract vocabulary items.
- Use dictionaries to make students understand the meaning of unknown vocabulary items.

Teaching vocabulary using communicative tasks

- **Organizing** graphics helps students to learn new vocabulary through authentic examples and **visual representation.**

- **Using graffiti** vocabulary when the words are associated with specific concepts. Teachers can make students create word posters by transforming the students' work into the class word wall.

- Using the **word wall** match-up strategies can help students to use problem solving and reasoning skills to match up terms with definitions, and in some cases symbolic representation.

- Giving students an opportunity to create a **prefix reference chart** in their notes. A quick activity at the beginning of the school year can help students breakdown new words based on their understanding of prefixes and root words.

- Using **word splash which** is a collection of key words or concepts chosen from a passage or chapter that students are about to read. This strategy gives students a chance to relate the new words or concepts to the main topic of the reading.

3. Teaching pronunciation

In the process of communication, pronunciation is of paramount importance, since successful communication cannot take place without correct pronunciation (Celce-Murcia, Brinton, and Goodwin, 1996). Pronunciation contains the role of individual sounds and sound segments, as well as super segmental features such as stress, rhythm, and intonation. In recent studies, suggestions have been made to develop materials addressing the communicative, psychological, sociocultural dimension of pronunciation.

PPP framework can be used for a lesson that teaches pronunciation. A PPP lesson is divided into three stages: Presentation, Practice, and Production. The teacher presents and teaches new language to the students by demonstrating it to them, explaining it and providing students with a lot of practice in how it can be used. By the end of the lesson, during the Production phase, the new language becomes part of the students' own knowledge of language and they should be able to use it easily and correctly.

Presentation

1. Introducing the new pronunciation features
2. Imitating the pronunciation of the new feature several times
3. Describing the way of producing new feature through oral or written illustrations
4. Comparing and contrasting the new feature in L1 and L2
5. Familiarizing learners with the new feature through sufficient exposure

Practice

1. **One of the biggest obstacles in clear pronunciation is vowel length.** Short vowels aren't short enough and long vowels aren't long enough. Ask students to practice contrasting exercises where long vowels are extra-long (e.g. 'seeeeeat') and short vowels are very short (e.g. 'sit').

2. **Explicit instruction in how to position the mouth while speaking helps learners cope with difficult sounds.** First, show with videos and exaggerate making the sounds yourself. Then pass out mirrors and ask students to observe their own mouth positions while forming the sounds.

21

3. **You ask students to hear the listening part before they come to the classroom.** Encourage students to get as much listening experience outside of the classroom as possible.

4. **Tongue twisters are a great way to practice pronunciation, but instead of doing all the work, share the load with your students.** Making students create their own tongue twisters helps them not only practice their pronunciation, but also be more aware of which sounds are in the words they know.

5. **Students need to get feedback early and often before they get used to bad pronunciation that are difficult to change as later learners.** As a teacher, it can be difficult to manage a large classroom and give individualized pronunciation feedback to many students. A good way to maintain a large classroom is to make notes while students are speaking, for example during role plays or individual presentations to know the biggest pronunciation problems.

6. **It is good to do stress marking activities.** You can give students a list of words they already know and ask them to identify stressed and unstressed syllables until they understand the idea of stress.

7. **English has incredibly unpredictable word stress patterns which are rather difficult to learn because of all of the exceptions to the rules.** The best way to learn word stress is to practice as you introduce new vocabulary words.

Production

Listening and repeating, filling in the blanks, and communicative practice to involve learners in attending to both form and content of utterances are considered as useful ways to control students' production. Young learners are capable of developing great pronunciation skills; however, the older the learner gets, the more difficult it can be to have good pronunciation habits.

Some points in teaching pronunciation

- There is no superiority over British or American way of pronunciation. Intelligibility or comprehensibility is important.

- In order to draw students' attention, *teachers' pronunciation can be exaggerated* (**Enunciation:** pronouncing words or parts of words clearly which can be used as a technique in teaching pronunciation).
- There may not be a correspondence between the spelling and pronunciation of a word.
- Pronunciation is more important than phonetics for beginners.
- Stress and intonation are as important as the sounds themselves and should be taught from the very beginning.
- Beginners of English, especially young learners, should be avoided being taught phonetics.
- Efficiency is the realistic goals of teaching pronunciation.
- Recognition practice should precede production practice.
- Students should be given the opportunity to hear the same things said by more than one voice as the model.
- Advanced students need to be able to read International Phonetic Alphabets.
- Poor pronunciation may cause problems for the learning of other skills.
- Adult learners need to focus on pronunciation, but young learners don't.
- Both consistency and accuracy in pronunciation are very important.
- Students should learn Received Pronunciation (RP). (The standard accent of English)
- Stress in pronunciation is sometimes as important as grammar.
- Bad intonation can lead to serious misunderstandings.

Aspects of pronunciation

A broad definition of pronunciation contains both **suprasegmental** and **segmental** features. Although these different aspects of pronunciation are considered in isolation, it is important to remember that they all work in combination when we hear an utterance.

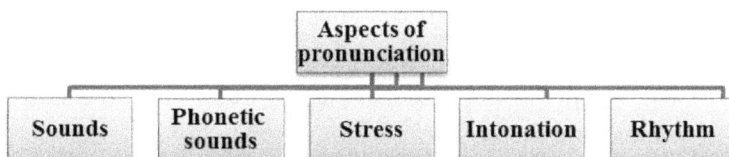

Figure 1.5 *Aspects of Pronunciation*

English consonants are different based on place of articulation, manner of articulation, or being voice/voiceless. Vowels are distinguished from each other by being monophthong (a pure vowel sound whose articulation at both beginning and end is relatively fixed) or diphthong (the vowel quality changes within the same syllable). Rhythm is a product of sentence stress and what happens to the words and sounds between the stresses. Teachers can work in groups and brainstorm the common problems that students of their country experience with English pronunciation. Then discuss the possible causes for these problems and possible solutions.

What do teachers need to know in teaching phonology?
- Knowledge of the pronunciation features including articulation rules
- Awareness of students' potential problems through diagnostic work
- Pedagogical importance including which features should be taught and when

The role of pronunciation
Factors that determine whether pronunciation needs special attention
- Learners' native language (different languages have different sound systems)
- Exposure to English (ESL/EFL has distinct features in acquiring the sound system of a new language)
- Age (young and adult learners acquire the phonetic system of a new language differently)
- Individual ability (biological and physical)

Factors for improving learners' pronunciation
- Imitation of teachers or recorded models of sounds
- Recording of learners' speech
- Systematic explanation and instruction about articulatory movement
- Varied speed, volume, mood imitation, and repetition drills as in repetition of sounds, words, and sentences chorally and individually
- learning and performing dialogues using choral work, and varied speed, volume, and mood
- Implementing jazz chants: simple way of learning with special attention to the sound system of the language with clapping and stamping to bring joy into the classroom

- Self-correction through listening to recordings of own speech
- Practicing famous tongue twisters (a phrase or sentence which is hard to recite fast because of a sequence of nearly similar sounds, e.g. (Sister Susie Sells Sea Shells on the Sea Shore.)
- Avoiding teaching English sounds individually
- Minimizing correction
- Using media to improve pronunciation
- Recording self-reading
- Listening to English music

Practicing Stress

Stress refers to the amount of force with which a sound or syllable is uttered. It is the only factor in making rhythmic differences.

Word stress: all words of more than one syllable have word stress. This means that at least one of the syllables is **louder** than the other syllables. Different parts of speech make different stressful syllabus.

> **PHO**tograph   pho**TO**graphy   photo**GRA**phic

In many cases, word stress must simply be learned when new vocabulary is acquired. However, there are several rules for word stress which can make it easier to deal with.

1. **Compound Nouns**: Keyboard

   In this example, the first part of the compound gets the stress.

2. **Noun + Noun compounds** (two-word compound nouns): French fry

   In this example, similar to the rule for compound nouns, the first part of the compound (the first word) gets the stress.

3. **Phrasal verbs** (two-part verbs) are generally made up of a verb and preposition. For many of these, correct word stress is especially important as they have compound noun counterparts. In the following examples, the words on the left are phrasal verbs while the words on the right are nouns.

   work out   workout   shut out   shutout

4. **Homographs** are words which are written the same way but which have different pronunciation. In English, there are many words

which have the same spelling, but whose part of speech changes with the word stress.

Verb	Noun
re**cord**	**re**cord
pro**gress**	**pro**gress

Sentence stress: it has no fixed distribution. It emphasizes the portion of the utterance that has more importance for the speaker.

Three ways to show stress
1. Using the voice to emphasize on the stressful syllabus through raising the voice
2. Using gestures to indicate the stressful syllabus through raising the hand
3. Using the board to mark the position of the stressful syllabus

Practicing intonation
Intonation is speech melody, the way our voice goes up and down in speaking. Intonation is very important in expressing meaning, and especially in showing our feelings, such as surprise, anger, disbelief, gratitude, etc. Intonation patterns are quite complex and it is better for students to acquire them naturally rather than consciously.

Basic types of intonation in questions
Falling intonation exists in wh- questions and statements while rising intonation exists in yes- no questions.

Concluding remarks
1. Use individual, pair, group and whole class work to create a pleasant, relaxed, and dynamic classroom.
2. Use gestures through moving around the classroom to conduct choral pronunciation practice.
3. Vary the criteria of "good" in pronunciation practice to give students confidence.
4. Use articulation practice more than once.
5. Bring interests and variety to the practice of pronunciation.
6. Rely on explanations and demonstrations simultaneously.
7. Try to use visual aids.
8. Be an imaginative and creative teacher.

9. Do not speak word by word.
10. Connect words to form sound groups.

Tasks in teaching intonation

Ask the following questions

- Listen to the words. "How many syllables do you hear?"
- Listen to the words. "Which syllable is stressed?"
- Do the questions "go up?" or "go down?"

Teaching language skill
(Listening, Speaking, Reading, and Writing)

1. Teaching listening

Listening is not a "passive" skill but an *"active"* skill. It requires as much attention and mental activity as speaking may need. Listening is crucial in the language classroom because it provides input for leaners. Without facing understandable input at the right level, learning can not begin. In listening classroom, teachers should give learners some degree of control over the content of the lesson. Students can be involved in the process of listening in the following ways:

- Teachers should make instructional goals completely explicit to learners.
- Teachers should give learners a degree of choice.
- Teachers should allow students to bring their background information into the classroom.
- Teachers should encourage students to develop skills and strategies to improve their listening ability.

Effective featueres of listening in the classroom

- The materials should be authentic.
- Content of listening should be personalised.
- Leamers should know the purpose of what they are listening to.
- The tasks should provide students with chance of getting an active role in their own learning.
- Materials should be incorporated with effective strategies.

When an individual is engaged in communicative learning situation, approximately 9% is devoted to writing, 16% to reading, 30% to speaking, and 45% to listening.

Principles of teaching listening

1. **Encourage students to have exposure to authentic recordings as much as possible.** The incorporation of authentic materials into a lesson can stimulate the classroom atmosphere and help foster a *positive attitude* toward learning (television programs, radio shows, and public announcements). *The audio player is just as important as the listening activity.* All

the appliances that are used in listening classroom must work properly to go backwards or forwards.

2. **Preparation is necessary.** Teachers and students need to be prepared for listening before they enter the class.

3. **Once is not enough.** Generally speaking, students are inclined to hear the listening part more than once to pick up the things they missed the first time.

4. **Teachers should encourage students to answer to content of a listening, not just to the language.** As with reading, the most important part of listening practice is to draw out the meaning, what is intended, and what impression it makes on the students.

5. **Different listening stages need different listening tasks.** Based on students' different listening stages, different tasks should be considered (from general understanding to detail information).

6. **Listening texts should be used to the full.** Teachers can be creative in using the listening tasks for as many applications as possible to change the role of listening from an exercise to an important event.

7. **Distinction between hearing and listening should be made.** Hearing is done by the ears while listening is done with the mind and the heart.

8. **Listening tasks should be carefully chosen.** Listening tasks with regard to text type based on oral text/ literate type, the length of the text, and the difficulty level of the text influence on the process of listening.

9. **The audio visual materials should not have a variety of accents at early stages of teaching listening.** Learners will get totally confused.

10. **The Audio visual materials should be used carefully.** Students will unconsciously omit the listening part and the entire exercise will be a failure. It is better to focus only on audio initially and gradually introduce audio visual.

The three phases in a listening lesson

Pre-listening stage: precedence of *grammar, conversation,* and *vocabulary* leads to motivation. Listening activity should never precede the above mentioned activities.

The purpose of the pre-listening stage is

- to prepare the learners for what they are going to hear.
- to activate existing knowledge through schema theory which focuses on the role of background knowledge in language comprehension.

- to introduc the language which students will encounter.
- to contextualize the text.
- to provide the learners with any necessary information about the setting and the role of participants.

Pre-listening activitis
- Predicting content from the title
- Describing the picture related to the text
- Discussing relevant experiences
- Talking about the topic
- Answering a set of questions about the topic
- Agreeing or disagreeing with students' opinions about the topic
- Associateing vocabulary with the topic
- Predicting information about the topic
- Writing questions about the topic

While-Listening Stage
The purpose of while-listening stage is
- to help learners understand the text.
- to make learners involved in an authentic and purposeful listening activity more intensively.

While-listening activities
- Ticking multiple-choice items
- Filling in a chart
- Completing a table, map or picture
- Matching pictures with the text
- Taking notes
- Answering questions
- Completing sentences

Post-listening stage
The purpose of post-listening activities is
- to help learners connect what they have heard with their own ideas and experience.
- to help learners to move easily from listening to another skill.

- to give opinions, to relate similar experiences, to play a similar interaction role, to write a brief report, to write a similar text, and to debate the topic.

Advantages of the above listening activities

- They personalize the lesson and make the listening interesting.
- They integrate listening with the other skills, especially speaking.

Teaching listening in practice

Listening exercises are usually taught in two main ways:

A: Do it in the classroom without prior preparation.

1. **Warm-up: brainstorm** and try to introduce the topic; **key words** can be treated.
2. **Listen once or twice without pause:** in order to get the main idea (listening for the gist)
3. **Play the audio program part by part and ask them to explain** (listening for details): audio program makes cheap and interactive educational activities for students that teachers cannot create.
4. **Discuss the topic if it is necessary:** evaluate students' comprehension by discussing the topic.

B: Assign it to be done at home. This method is much better:

1. **Assign the listening exercise** and let your students **transliterate** at home.
2. **Listen once** with no pause.
3. **Ask them** to give you **summary** or ask the **questions of the books** or give **details**.
4. **Play the audio program** part by part and ask them to **repeat** and **explain**.
5. **Discuss the topic** (if necessary).

There are two types of listening processes

Bottom-up processes: we use our knowledge of language and our ability to process acoustic signals to make sense of the sounds that speech presents to us by recognizing processing input, word divisions, key words, key transitions, gammatical elements, stress, and intonation to listen effectively.

Top-down processes: we infer meaning from contextual clues and from making links between the spoken message and various types of prior knowledge which we hold. This process can be activated through infering key words to make the schema of discourse, the role of the participants, the topic of a discourse, the cause and effect of an event, the sequence of events, and comparisons.

Tasks in listening comprehension

- **Listening to comprehend** is used in order to answer some comprehensive questions.
- **Listening to notice** is used to make learners focus on a specific feature of language such as grammatical points by filling in the missing words.
- **Listening to learn** is using contextual information to help learning unknown linguistic forms.
- **Listening to do tasks** is used to listen to directions to choose and place objects. It contains **"still-life task"** to arrange pictures of everyday objects such as books and notebooks, **"map task"** to show various locations such as hospitals and book stores, **"shapes task"** to represent diagrams of various geometrical shapes to number them on their picture sheets, and **"kitchen task"** to make learners listen to directions about placing different objects in a matrix picture of a kitchen.
- **Academic listening tasks** consist of lectures on academic topics. Listeners have to take some notes.

Key aspects of listening to comprehend

- The **purpose** of listening can be determined by the text itself. The purpose of listening to a text can influence what is listened and how it is listened.
- There are three different **roles for the listener**. The **over-hearer** whose participation is not important, the **addressee** who is directly addressed by the speaker, and the **hearer** who is not directly addressed. In task-based teaching all listeners have important functions in the process of listening and there is little place for over-hearers. A participant' role as listener affects comprehension.
- Using **schematic knowledge** refers to knowledge of the world and knowledge of the ways textual information is organized to comprehend a text for interpretation, prediction, and hypothesis testing. Interpretation means recognizing important lexical items.

Prediction can be made based on interpretation. Hypothesis testing needs more processing of text language to accept or reject prediction.

- Using **contextual knowledge** that is available to listeners as they are functioning as listeners.
- **Mental model of collaborative construction** in interactive listening tasks means listeners are more successful in comprehension when they have shared mental model with speakers.

Teaching listening using communicative tasks

- Teachers can play recorded talk shows, stories, sports commentary, news, etc.
- Some questions based on the conversation can be asked and the class should be split into groups. Do not take conversations which go beyond ten minutes to start with.
- Ask the groups to answer the questions and make it a competition.
- Teachers can also introduce a lot of listening games.
- Depending on the class strength, ask each student to find details about any 5 parameters, which you can decide by talking to the other class members. The 5 parameters could be father's age, favorite dish, favorite color, date of birth and ambition.
- Make it clear to the students that they cannot note down anything.
- Make a time limit. Ask the students or the groups to come out and share the details they have gathered about other class members. Ensure that you ask each student to write down their answers before you start the game and give it to you.
- Award a point for the right answer. Ensure no student or team notes down anything. They should not talk between themselves when the game starts. The beauty of this game is the bonding that can be created within the participants apart from the fun factor.

2. Teaching speaking and conversation

Teaching speaking

Learning to speak English requires more than knowing its grammar and semantic system. Learners must learn the knowledge of how native speakers use English in the context of structured interpersonal exchange fluently and appropriately.

Some important points in improving speaking skill in the classroom

The success of a speaking lesson depends primarily on the following factors:

Teachers: they must be trained and also be enthusiastic about teaching.

Activities: they should be planned in advance based on careful instruction.

Language: it is important to supply key language elements to carry out speaking activities.

Topics: they are supposed to activate students' schemata meaningfully.

Motivation: it gets students to be involved in what they are doing.

How to teach students to speak English

For an effective speaking lesson, teachers need to be aware of, knowledgeable about, and familiar with the *teaching stages* of a speaking activity as well as the *teaching techniques* used for fostering speaking in class. Also, the *teacher's role* is crucial to the effectiveness of the activity.

Teaching stages for a speaking activity

a) Pre-communicative stage

b) Practice stage

c) Communicative interaction or production stage

During the pre-communicative stage

- Introduce the communicative function.
- Highlight the fixed expressions.
- Point out the target structure.
- Provide students with the necessary vocabulary.
- Provide students with the language of interaction.

During the practice stage

- Correct students *if necessary*. It should be considered that error correction while focusing on fluency is not suggested.

- Prompt students if necessary (do it lexically) through communicative activities to increase participation in speaking activities.
- Aim for intelligibility through expressing thoughts, feelings, and getting involved in real-life communication.

During the communicative interaction
- Encourage language negotiation.
- Take note of any aspects that may hinder communication (pronunciation, vocabulary, grammar).
- Respect students' "wait" time.
- Give students *feedback* on their pronunciation, grammar, and vocabulary. *Then ask them to repeat the task if necessary.*

Role-plays: students are given a specific role and have to make a conversation.

A: You're a tourist in New York downtown. You need to find your way to the nearest restaurant. Ask a pedestrian for directions.

B: You live in New York. You're stopped by a tourist. Give him/her directions.

During a speaking lesson a teacher can be a/an

organizer to keep students engaged in activities.

prompter to provide students with chunks not words.

observer to analyze what causes communication breakdowns.

participant to not monopolize or initiate the conversation.

assessor to record mental or written samples of language produced by students.

Feedback provider to tell students how proficient their performance was.

resource to provide students with tools to improve their oral performance.

What should teachers do during a speaking activity?

It is considered that teachers should not dominate during speaking activities. Students appreciate teacher participation at the appropriate level. Teachers have the role of facilitators while someone in a role-play can't think of what to say, they will have to intervene in some way if the activity is not going smoothly, or if a discussion begins to dry up. Prompting is often necessary but, as with correction, teachers should do it sympathetically and sensitively.

The main goal of an English language course
- To focus on developing students' mastery of the language form
- To focus on developing students' ability to communicate effectively for study, work, or leisure

Features of using language for communication
- We communicate because we want to or need to, *not* just to practice the language.
- Focus should be placed on *what* we are communicating *not* on *how* we are communicating (ideas vs. language).
- The language that is used is *varied* in grammar and vocabulary, it shoud *not* be made of a single structure or a few structures and it should *not* be repeated over and over again.

Communication in the classroom
- Establish English as the main classroom language to encourage real communication.
- Try to use interesting topics and stimulating activities, which take the learners' minds off the language.
- Bring real life events (weather, the students' clothes, their health, mood, pictures,and realia) to class.
- Talk about events in the world outside (new films, a circus in town, national sports victory, the students' families, etc.).
- Focus on fluency vs. accuracy to support and encourage listeners in their efforts to communicate their ideas.
- Don't try to control what they say. Correct global errors rather than local errors.
- Don't interrupt learners everytime when they make a language mistake in order to correct them.
- Don't choose *too easy or too difficult tasks,* the students may become *demotivated.*
- Avoid frustration and fatigue by using different speaking activities.
- Ban mother-tongue application in speaking.

Familiarize your students with some important communication strategies

- **Avoidance Strategies:** when speaking or writing a second/foreign language, a speaker will often try to avoid using a difficult word or structure, and use a simpler word or structure instead. This is called avoidance strategy.

- **Compensatory strategies**
  a) **Circumlocution:** describing the target object
  b) **Approximation:** using an alternative term
  c) **Prefabricated:** using memorized phrases
  d) **Appeal for help:** asking for help in speaking

Common characteristics of successful speaking tasks

Maximize foreign talk: try to avoid students' talking in the mother tongue, and avoid too much Teacher Talk.

Balance participation: try to avoid outstanding students' dominating discussions. Try to guarantee equal opportunities for students of different levels.

Make high motivation: bring interesting topics and clear objectives into the class. Make sure that the task is in line with the students' ability.

Consider right language level: the task must be designed so that the students can complete the task successfully with the language that they have. Otherwise the task will become frustrating and the students are likely to give up or revert to the native language.

Teaching language function (Conversation)
The importance of conversation in EFL

Conversation exercises are meant to introduce a specific communicative function (ordering food, making a phone call, asking for prices, etc.). They present new grammar structures in a situational and communicative context. They introduce new vocabulary in context and they make good pronunciation models.

The steps for handling conversations in practice

1. **Warm-up:** there are different ways for having a warm-up, including **brainstorming, asking for students' opinions, personal experience and suggestions, localizing the topic, etc.** It's also a good idea to put **the title on the board.**

2. **Picture description:** students look at the picture and talk about the things they see in the picture that accompanies the conversation.

3. **Playing the recording:** students listen to get general information from the conversation.

4. **Playing the recording again:** students are asked to check their understanding.

5. **Explanation and paraphrasing interactively:** students open their books and, with the help of their teacher, clarify new vocabulary items, functions, expressions, and grammatical points.
   New words and expressions should be written on the board.

6. **Working on phonological aspects:** students repeat chorally and individually after the teacher or the audio program. Students should work both on word *stress* and on *intonation*.

7. **Pair-work:** each student works with *a partner* and imitates the conversation using the same words. Students should practice using *the look up and say technique*, rather than "reading" over the text. You can encourage students to use *gestures*.

8. **Personalization of the conversation:** students practice the dialog again, this time changing it using *their personal information*. Then 1 or 2 pairs *act out* their changed conversation in front of the class.

9. **Assignment:** the teacher can have students:
   - Make sentences using new words of the conversation.
   - Make questions about the conversation.
   - Summarize or reproduce the conversation using the grammar box and new words.

Note: Avoid too much analysis over listening script. This does not serve any useful purpose for improving listening per se. However, it is good to expand new vocabulary items through listening exercises.

Interactive tasks in teaching speaking and conversation

Interactive tasks make learners involved in interpersonal interaction. They contain the **negotiation** of meaning, **communicative strategies**, and **communicative effectiveness**.

- The **negotiation** of meaning can be received through four strategies.
  1- **Comprehension checks** to show whether the speaker's utterance has been understood, for example, *Do you know what I mean?*
  2- **Clarification requests** elicit clarification of the preceding utterance, for example:
  A: *I am really pleased.*
  B: *Uh?*
  A: *I am happy.*
  3- **Confirmation checks** confirm the preceding speaker's utterance, for example:
  A: *I am really pleased.*
  B: *You are happy?*
  A: *Yes.*
  4- **Recasts** change one or more components of a sentence while referring to its central meanings, for example:
  A: *I went shopping.*
  B: *You went shopping. What did you buy?*
  A: *A bag.*

- **Communication strategies** are employed when speakers have to communicate meanings when they do not have enough linguistic knowledge. There are different examples of communication strategies. 1- **Reduction strategies** (topic avoidance, message abandonment, and meaning replacement) are used when learners abandon specific messages. 2- **Achievement strategies**
  a- Lexical substitution for example:
  My uncle is the president of junior high school.
  ("president" = principal)
  b- Generalization for example:

Eh... I... went to... uh... the port to Kish Island, ah! We   need two days.
("went" = sailed)

   c- Exemplification for example:

So, it is good way for the sport ah... sports ah... people to ah...   eat ah...bread or rice or spaghetti... something like that. (= carbohydrates)

   d- Circumlocution (paraphrase or description) for example:

A: *What kind of work.*

B: *Oh, oh.. I was working now eh... Develop and...fine-   line   pattern, (laugh) uh... circuit board,*

like circuit board... very fine.

A: *Uh huh...*

B: *Uh... fine line, and... very very narrow.. line... On a board.*

A: *So, it's a new... new kind of IC or something like...*

B: *No no no no... circuit board, full circuit board...*

IC is settled on this.. circuit (= surface-mount technology)

   e- Word   coinage for example:

And... at the mountain, we... get off the
taxi, and.. climb... the mountain. It
takes.... in total we have we are.. we
stayed... two... sleep..... s::leep days
in the mountain. ("sleep day" = night)

   f- Morphological creativity for example:

ah... we have to uh... uh..
internationalization, but.. before..
before that we have uh.. been
internationaliza-, internationalizated

   h- Language switch , i- foreignizing, j- literal translation, etc. are used when learners keep communication by   compensating   for insufficient means for achieving it.

- **Communicative effectiveness** represents *identification of referent dimension* to encode the referents in tasks of "spot-the-difference" and "narrative tasks". Here speakers need three kinds of ability (perceptual, comparison, and linguistic ability), *the role taking dimension* is about the ability of the participants to recognize the other speaker's perspective and feedback.

3. Teaching reading

In many language situations, reading receives a special focus. Many students consider reading as one of their most important goals to be able to read for information and pleasure, for their career, and for study purposes. Written texts serve various pedagogical purposes. Extensive exposure to comprehensible written texts can enhance the process of language learning. Good reading texts also provides good models for writing, stimulating new topics for discussion, and studying language (e.g., vocabulary, grammar, and idioms).

Purposes for reading in academic settings
- To search for information
- To get general comprehension
- To learn new information
- To synthesize and evaluate information

Principles of reading comprehension
- Good teachers optimize a reading text to the full. They believe all children can learn, differentiate instruction using a variety of techniques and strategies, know that students learn best in authentic situations, have profound knowledge of reading; provide lots of opportunities for students to read, and repeatedly use assessment evidence to fine-tune instruction.
- Explicitly teaching different reading comprehension strategies creates students' reasoning power. These contain previewing, self-questioning, making connections, visualizing, knowing how words work, monitoring (Does this make sense?), summarizing, and evaluating.
- Vocabulary improvement is necessary. It is developed by increasing students' interest in learning and using new words, using precision in word use, getting students actively involved in the process, studying how words work, exposing students to new words multiple times, and developing vocabulary development in other subject areas.
- Motivation is an important factor. Effective teachers make students interested in reading by creating an appropriate environment, making compelling texts available, and creating intrinsic motivation.
- It is suggested to push students to comprehend at deeper levels. Students need to go beyond passively accepting a text's

41

message and read between and beyond the lines. Thinking about the author's purpose and the underlying message of the text should be considered.

- Continually, the teachers should check for understanding. Teachers should observe students as they read and discuss, look at their informal written responses, use other assessments, and gain insights to follow up and fine-tune instruction.

- Students should use different ways to represent their thinking. Oral and written responses are good, but students should also be able to sketch, dramatize, sing, and create projects about their reading.

- Students should read different types and levels of text. They include instructional-level books and easier texts for independent reading.

- Reading comprehension is the active construction of meaning as the reader makes connections between prior knowledge and the text.

- Students should be stimulated to respond to the content of the reading text. They should get involved in what they are reading and match the task to the topic.

Reading skills

1. **Skimming:** readers skim a text when they look it over quickly to get a general idea of the subject matter.
2. **Scanning:** readers scan a piece of writing when they quickly search for specific information.
3. **Intensive reading:** you read with concentration and great care in order to understand exactly the meaning of what you read. This is particularly necessary for legal documents, financial documents, academic reports and anything to do with business.
4. **Extensive reading:** you read as many different kinds of books/journals/papers as you can, chiefly for pleasure, and general understanding of the content.

The three phases in teaching reading
Pre-reading activity/the purposes of the pre-readingstage

- To introduce and stimulate interest in the topic
- To motivate students
- To improve top-down and bottom- up processing

While-reading activity/the purposes of the while-reading stage
- To clarify content, structure and vocabulary of the text
- To develop vocabulary (developing top-down processing)
- To increase reading comprehension (top-down and bottom-up processes)

Post-reading activity/the purposes of the post-readingstage
- To reflect upon what has been read and check understanding (outcome of the two processes)
- To relate the text to the students' own knowledge, interests, and views (speaking incitation)

Reading skill is manifested in some stages. It starts from utilizing the background knowledge, then clarifying the content, and finally expanding the learned materials.

What students know	What they want to know	What they have learned	How can they learn more?
1.	1.	1.	1.
2.	2.	2.	2.
3.	3.	3.	3.
4.	4.	4.	4.
5.	5.	5.	5.

Table 1.1 *A Reading Activity Scheme*

Teaching reading in practice
The steps for teaching a passage are as follows:

Pre-reading
1. **Warm-up**: the reading is started using a warm-up (Books closed). This can be done by:
- Brainstorming
- Asking some general questions
- Asking for personal experience, etc.

2. **Writing the title on the board**: the title of the passage is put on the board. Students then give **their ideas** about the title and try to guess the content of the passage.
3. **Picture description**: students open their books and describe what they see

in the picture. This part should be relevant to the topic of the passage.

4. **Silent reading**: students are given 3 or 5 minutes to quickly skim the passage to understand the main ideas of the text. Then the teacher selects 1 or 2 students (or *volunteers*) to say what the text is about and what it wants to discuss.

While-reading

1. **Explanation and paraphrasing**: during this part of the procedure, the teacher reads over the text aloud and stops to paraphrase any expressions which are not clear (which should be done interactively and with the help of students).

   - **All new vocabulary should be put on the board.** Once the text has been covered you can make the students repeat the new words and make sentences with them.
   - **Vocabulary in reading:** at first try to invite the students to make good guesses about the meaning of the words. Then, give students simple synonyms and explanations.

2. **Defining the task**: the teacher guides students towards the questions of the passage and gives them instruction on how to complete the task.

3. **Completing the task:** students are supposed to scan the text during this stage in order to answer the questions of the passage and complete the task.

4. **Comparing answers**: here, students are given some time to check their answers in pairs, after which several are selected to read their answers aloud to the whole class.

Post-reading

This step involves discussing the passage and giving personal opinions.

   - Make jumbled paragraphs (cohesion and coherence).
   - Cut up the text into paragraphs.
   - Ask students to reconstruct the text by putting the paragraphs into the appropriate/right order.

Assignment: students can be asked to

   - make sentences with the new words.
   - make questions about the passage, or prepare a summary.
   - do extensive reading (reading material other than the passages in the book).

Fluent readers usually do the followings

- They read rapidly for comprehension.
- They recognize words automatically.
- They depend on a very large stored vocabulary.
- They integrate text information with their own knowledge.
- They recognize the purpose of the reading.
- They comprehend the text when it is necessary.
- They change purposes to read strategically.
- They use strategies to increase comprehension.
- They repair miscomprehension.

Teaching reading using communicative tasks

- Ask the students to read the chosen text carefully.
- Prepare a chart based on the text and ask students to fill in the chart. They can write "no" if they do not have information.
- Make some true or false questions. Ask them to put a tick into the correct place.
- Write some questions and ask them to respond to the questions.
- Make some definitions and ask the students to guess the word (the words are from the text).
- Make some questions and ask them to answer orally to the questions.
- Ask them to read the text again. Then write a composition about themselves. They can use the text to help them.

4. Teaching writing

There are several ways to approach writing in the classroom. A product approach is a traditional approach, in which students are encouraged to copy a model text, which is usually presented and analyzed at an early stage. Process approaches to writing tend to focus more on the varied classroom activities which promote the development of language use such as brainstorming, group discussion, and re-writing. In the communicative framework of language teaching, the skill of writing enjoys special attention. Such communication is extremely important in the modern world to interact traditionally (paper-and-pencil writing) or technologically (advanced electronic mail). Writing as a communicative activity needs to be supported and nurtured during language learning process.

Stages in teaching the process of writing

Teachers often plan classroom activities that support the learning of specific writing skills at every stage. These planned learning experiences are as follows:

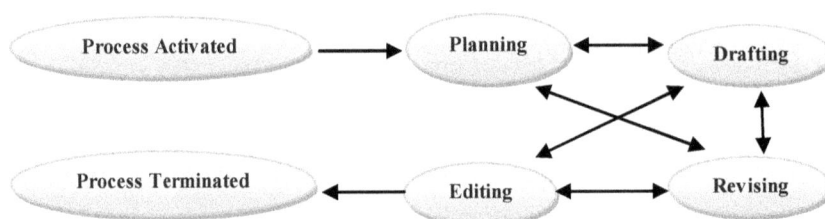

Figure1.6 *Writing process (Adapted from Richards & Renandya, 2000, p.315)*

Pre-writing (Planning)

It is an activity in the classroom that encourages students to write. It stimulates thinking to start writing.

Group brainstorming: group members express their ideas about topic. Spontaneity is the key factor.

Clustering: students form words related to a stimulus supplied by the teacher. The words come in circles then linked by lines.

Rapid free writing: within 1 or 2 minutes, students write down single words and phrases about a topic.

Wh-question: students make *who, why, what, when,* and *how* questions and then they answer to them.

Writing

Drafting: when sufficient ideas are collected at the planning stage, it is time to draft at this stage. The writers are focused on the fluency of writing rather than grammatical accuracy.

Responding: the teacher or peers can respond to students' writing. Responding is a stage between drafting and revising and it should not be done in the final stage.

Revising: the students reexamine what was written to see how appropriately they have expressed their meanings to the readers.

Editing: at this stage, students are involved in tidying up their writing as they prepare the final draft to be evaluated by the teacher.

Evaluating: in order to be effective, the criteria for evaluation should be made known to students in advance.

Post-writing

It consists of any classroom activity that the teacher and the students can do with the completed form of writing.

How to help students improve their writing skills: ask them

- not to overuse passive voice.
- to use strong and precise words.
- to write in a clear, simple, and direct way.
- to edit, edit, edit.
- to read and understand the works of great and influential writers.
- to read magazines, newspapers, and everything else.
- to write every day.
- to pick a topic and lay out a general arc for it.
- to write an outline.
- not to plagiarize.

Some reasons for teaching writing

1. **Reinforcing:** some students acquire languages in an oral/aural way, but most students prefer written form of language.
2. **Development of language:** complex mental activities are needed to construct proper written texts in learning experience.
3. **It is a learning style:** in accordance with learning styles, students are different in picking up languages. Writing is suitable for reflective and intrapersonal students who have difficulties in face-to-face activities.
4. **It's a language skill:** the most important reason to teach writing is that it is one of the four basic language skills. Writing is needed to write letters, reports, emails, etc. Students need to be taught writing conventions (punctuation, and paragraph construction).

Writing activities for different levels

For elementary levels writing activities are usually restricted to sentence-making, grammar practices, correct real mistakes, and fill the gaps in a text and then write a composition. *For intermediate levels* writing is more content-based i.e., writing about their own lives and childhood memories, mistake correction, a gap-fill text, and a composition. *For advanced levels* students should have both look and content in mind. They are supposed to be able to make academic writing, write a letter to an editor, and provide job application.

What kind of writing should students do?

Like other aspects of English teaching, the type of writing activities should be based on students' age, interest, and level.

Age: beginners can start with simple poems. An extended report is not an appropriate task for them.

Interest: a writing assignment should be presented based on students' interests. Find out why students are registered in the course, how they feel about the subject matter, and what their expectations are.

Level: considering how much language the students know is an important factor in selecting appropriate writing assignment.

What can be done about handwriting?

Based on Harmer (2007), handwriting is considered very personal. It reflects an individual's character. But it's an important skill because it makes visual memory and develops visual recall, which is critical for effective reading skills. Unless children recognize the differences in letters instantly, they are not going to be good readers. Teachers aren't in a position to ask students to change their handwriting style, but they can insist on *legibility* and *neatness*.

How can classmates help?

Whatever type of text teachers ask students to produce, peer correction can be a very useful part of the process. Peer correction often helps to create a positive class atmosphere as students realize teachers are not the only source of error correction and they can learn a lot from one another. Divide students into some groups and ask them to exchange papers within each group. Students should be asked to comment on each other's papers within group work. Look at all papers and comments to revise papers.

Correcting writing
What should teachers consider while correcting writing?

A. Look (appearance)

Capitaliztion refers to calitalizing the first letters of every new sentene, proper names, pronoun *I*, etc.

1- **Margine lines are used to** indent the first lines of paragraphs one half-inch from the left margin.
2- **Format** contains *Introduction, Body,* and *Conclusion* sections.
3- **Handwriting** should be readable, clear, and neat.
4- **Orthography** deals with rules of spelling.

5- **Punctuation** marks indicate the structure and organization of writing, as well as intonation and pauses to be observed when reading.

B. Content

1- **Word meaning** deals with choosing and using particular words in order to write appropriately.
2- **Grammar** refers to being able to use the best grammatical structures in writing.
3- **Unity** (oneness) is the essential quality of a paragraph. A paragraph is supposed to have a central idea, and everything in the paragraph relates to and develops that idea.
4- **Cohesion** (go togetherness) concerns the flow of sentences and paragraphs from one to another. It involves connecting old information to new information.
5- **Coherence** (fitness of parts) refers to the unity made between the ideas, sentences, paragraphs and different sections of a piece of writing.

Teachers have to achieve a balance in writing correction between being accurate and truthful on the one hand and treating students sensitively and sympathetically on the other hand.

- Determining the aspect of writing correction (punctuation, spelling, or grammar) should be considered. This has some advantages:
    1. It makes students concentrate on that particular aspect.
    2. It cuts down on the correction.
- Making a list of written symbols to be used when they come across a mistake in the margin or under the wrong word. (S= spelling, WO= word order, etc.).
- Correcting is important, but it can be time-consuming and frustrating. Common sense and talking to students about general mistakes are the solutions here.
- Corrected writing is important only if the students understand it before throwing it away. The teacher should ask the students to redraft the passage correctly.

Teachers can use some written comments range from *"Great"* to *"The story is interesting but it needs more attention"* to identify students' mistakes. After identifying the categories of the mistakes e.g. grammar, punctuation, etc. teachers can refer students to some useful books or sites to gain more information about their mistakes.

Current research findings

The weakness of applying certain teaching methods has led to teach a particular form of the language in non-authentic manner, setting, and practices. Care must be taken when teachers follow a strategy-based approach to teaching language skills and components. Once the strategies in question are taught, the learners are then required to do a lot of authentic tasks and practices, in which, it is hoped that they will apply the strategy-instruction that they have received. A strategy-based approach to teaching language skills and components is not new. However, it does ensure that in language learning courses learners are actually taught "how to" listen, read, write, and speak.

Conclusion

In this chapter, teaching language components including vocabulary, grammar, pronunciation and language skills containing listening, speaking, reading, and writing have been discussed.

Because of the importance of linguistic structure in second or foreign language learning, the role of grammar instruction should be taken into consideration. Three-dimensional grammar framework, the relation between grammar and second language learning, teaching grammar using communicative tasks, and guidelines on preparing new grammatical structures for teachers based on PPP and communicative approaches have been mentioned in this chapter.

Teaching vocabulary through incidental, intentional, and independent approaches needs a lot of effort in planning and wide variety of activities and exercises. The amount of emphasis to place on each activity depends on the learners' level and the educational goals. The steps for teaching vocabulary in practice and teaching vocabulary using communicative tasks should not be ignored.

In the field of language teaching, perspectives on the importance of teaching pronunciation are at variance. New suggestions are made to develop materials encompassing more communicative, psychological, and sociological aspects of pronunciation. Teaching pronunciation through PPP approach, aspects of pronunciation components, the teachers ' knowledge of teaching phonology, the role of pronunciation in communication, factors for improving learners' pronunciation, and practicing stress and intonation have been considered in this chapter.

Many ESL materials cannot provide learners with sufficient authentic data to use real English. Listening activities in English classroom should increase students' bottom-up and top-down listening skills. Students need to be exposed to substantial effective materials. It is essential to be aware of the fact that understanding every word does not suffice. Effective featueres of listening in the classroom, principles of teaching listening, the three phases in a listening lesson, teaching listening in practice, and tasks in listening comprehension are important factors to teach listening skill to students.

Speaking activities should be designed to provoke speaking as a skill to provide opportunities for rehearsal. Students should be motivated and encouraged to produce language automatically and autonomously. Decision-making, role-play, and interview "game" are supposed to be the most integral elements of speaking activities. Teaching stages for speaking activities, teachers' roles during speaking lessons, communication in the classroom, communication strategies, teaching language function (conversation), and interactive tasks in teaching speaking and conversation can improve students' speaking ability.

It is believed that the more students read, the better they get at reading. Reading is good for acquiring language. Teachers should encourage learners to read in a variety of ways extensively and intensively. The language of the text should be authentic-like to be used in skimming, and scanning. Principles of reading, reading skills, the three phases in teaching reading, ways to improve reading comprehension, and teaching reading through communicative tasks shape learners' reading skill.

Writing makes an opportunity for learners to learn language in a more focused way than speaking. Although writing process is important, grammatical inaccuracies have negative effects on the quality of writing. Therefore, teachers should help students improve their writing along with composing skills. Teachers ought to consider the role of classmate help, correcting writing, teaching writing stages, reasons for teaching writing, writing activities for different levels, and the importance of handwriting to improve students' writing skills.

CHAPTER TWO

Classroom English, Games, Tasks, and Techniques for Different Learners

"Be a student as long as you still have something to learn, and this will mean all your life". Henry L. Doherty

Introduction

In many countries, second language learning used to be mostly a secondary school program but there has been a definite trend towards teaching primary learners at lower and lower ages. It is believed that the younger you start, the more chance you have to make learning successful. If there is a critical age up to which acquiring a new language is easier and after that it is much more difficult to then it makes sense to focus attention on this issue.

Adults are not less successful in learning a new language. Studies have shown that adults enable to be better in a number of aspects of language learning. They can use abstract processes to learn grammatical points faster. Their higher intellect in the class leads to learning and retaining more vocabulary. Their maturity makes struggling with new language learning.

English teachers should consider that variable of age is an important factor in language learning. Children, teens and adults they need particular choice of language, techniques, lesson organization, and supporting materials. So, **level adaptation** should be taken into consideration.

Young learners
Characteristics of young learners

- Children are keen, noisy, and curious to learn new things. They love fun and attention.
- They can't be calm and can't concentrate for a long time.
- Children don't like to study the language. But they like to use it.
- Children may not see the point of language. But they see the point of interesting games and activities.
- Children can focus on the immediate *here and there*. Therefore, they need interest in their activities.
- Children need an animated, lively, and enthusiastic teacher.
- Children have a lot of curiosity.

Affective factors for young learners

Children are very sensitive and they have many inhibitions.

- Help children to laugh together in case of making mistake.
- Be supportive to make self-esteem.
- Make children participate in oral activities as much as possible.

Children learning based on authenticity and meaningfulness

Children cannot tolerate overload of impractical language learning. They enjoy tangible aspects of language. Teaching children should be context embedded with meaningful purposes far from abstract and isolated sentences.

Techniques for teaching English to children

1. **Use games and puzzles:** they lead to better learning. With **games,** students have fun in their classroom **activities.**
2. **Use flashcards:** they can improve students' imagination, memory, etc.
3. **Use interesting colors: color** plays a vitally **important** role in the class in which we teach. Teachers can use interesting colors for markers, pens, pencils, books, etc.
4. **Use songs actively:** it can make students enthusiastic and help them learn new words better.
5. **Use Fun:** children learn English when it is fun.
6. **Move away very slowly and with repetition:** young children are developing skills in their first language. So teachers should move away very slowly with a lot of repetition.
7. **Make use of realia:** use flash cards, pictures, objects.
8. **Review the taught materials every session:** it is good to *review* often throughout the course to keep *material* fresh in students' mind.
9. **Use words such as *Very good, Thank you, Listen, Repeat, Well done,* and *Come to the board please*:** excellent manners can help you to have better relationships with students you know, and those you will meet.
10. **Use as many gestures as possible:** lively gestures give learners a chance to experiment creatively the new acquired language so they can communicate meaningfully in real-life situations.

11. **Use total physical response:** this method is good for children but communicative method is good for adults through providing students with opportunities to focus on their own learning process.

12. **Don't use mechanical repetition:** games and puzzles keep students happy and interested. E.g. flash cards, games, and problem solving techniques can develop students' social relations so their motivation to study a foreign language can increase rapidly.

13. **Tell stories:** stories should be used with lots of pictures, gestures, facial expressions, mime, puppets and toys.

14. **Do practical tasks:** they can be painting, coloring, and making things but with instructions and help in English.

15. **Have more than one student at the board at the same time:** it means more students can participate in activities.

16. **Decrease distance (proximity) with your students:**
    - The major challenge is the first day of new term.
    - They come to English class for their very first lesson and class in English.
    - In general, women are better teachers for children.

17. **Provide learners with worksheets and activities to teach conversation:** they make **students** talk about a variety of topics to stimulate a long discussion on the **worksheet** topic during the **speaking lesson**.

18. **Ask parents to help:** parents, even with a basic knowledge of English, can successfully support their children to learn English.

How long should a lesson be? How much should we teach?

The amount of time that it may take a class to complete the assigned work might vary from class to class. Remember that this is also the case in teaching English language. You should consider the age and the level of students. Don't flood students with many items and don't make them bored.

Teaching the Alphabet

Learning the letters and sounds of English alphabet creates the foundational skills needed for understanding written language. Children who are learning to read first need to recognize, names, and connect their letters to sounds. You can teach the alphabet to children by using a variety of activities.

1- Tell your students that there are *two types of letters*. Ask them to repeat after you e.g. *"Big A"* and *"small a"*.

2- Show them the flash cards and use examples e.g. *"a"* like *"an apple"*.

3- Use patterns like: *"What's this?"* or *"Show me a small a"* while teaching letters.

4- Ask your students to play the role of the teacher and ask these questions.

5- Shuffle flash cards and ask them to match small and big letters.

6- Use *workbook* to practice alphabet. The *direction* of writing the alphabet is important.

7- *Review* the alphabet on the board every session.

8- Try to teach vowels before consonants.

Teaching vocabulary to children

1- Use *pictures*, *gestures* and avoid using mother tongue equivalent. Gestures and pictures are helpful for many classroom situations and applying them assists both you and your students. Do not necessarily use certain gestures. Do what comes naturally and when you find what works for you, stick with it to make your students adapt it.

2- Show them the pictures and ask them to repeat after you.

Teacher: *pen*
Students: *pen*
Teacher: *It's a pen*
Students: *It's a pen.*
Teacher: *What's this?*
Students: *It's a pen.*

3- Put some pictures on the board or on the desk and ask them to show you the objects.

Teacher: *Show me a book*
Student: *It's a book.*

4- Do interesting activities. You put can something in your bag and ask your students to touch it and guess what it is.

5- Ask students to unscramble the letters and make words. E.g. *g d o* →
dog

6- Use drawing. E.g. draw a cat on the board and say: *What's this?*

7- Use pantomime and ask your students to guess the job, action, etc. E.g. act out examining the patients.

8- Ask your students to do what you say. Say: *sit down, stand up,* etc.

Correction in English classes for children

Avoid overcorrection. Try to encourage them with positive correction. Young children look for their parents' praise. They need to feel good, and know they are making progress in English. In the early stages of learning, encouragement is especially important and praise for any small success motivates learners. E.g. *that's good*, *I like that*, and *well done*.

Teaching conversation to children

Useful patterns	Useful expressions
	Pardon me?
Teacher: What's this?	Excuse me?
Student: It's a book.	Hello everyone.
Student A: Hello, I am John.	Hi, how are you?
Student B: Hello, I am Sandra.	Sorry.
Teacher: What color is this?	I'm fine.
Student: It's red.	May I go out?
Teacher: What's your name?	(Are you speaking to) me?
Student: I am Bob.	Again, please.
Teacher: How old are you?	Be quiet. /Stop talking.
Student: I am six.	Don't do that.
Student A: I have a cat.	Let's start.
Student B: I have a dog.	Clap.
Teacher: How many books?	(Are you) Ready?
Student: Two.	Pencils down.
Teacher: What are you doing?	In English please.
Student: I am clapping.	Who's absent today?
Teacher: What time is it?	Look at page/ part/ number ~.
Student: It's five o'clock.	Sit down / Be seated.
Teacher: Where is the pencil?	Speak out.
Student: It's on the desk.	Stand up.
Teacher: Is Bob sitting?	Close your books/ notebooks.
Student: No, he is standing.	Good morning (class/ everyone).
Teacher: Is this a book?	Good afternoon (class/ everyone).
Student: Yes, it is.	That's all for today.
Teacher: Where do you live?	Goodbye.
Student: On Rose Street.	See you tomorrow/next week/Friday.
Teacher: What's wrong?	Who knows (the answer)?
Student: I am cold.	Come here.
Teacher: Whose pen is this?	Come in.
Student: It's Sandra's.	Go out.
Teacher: Show me your head.	Open the door.
Student: This is my head.	I like apples/ oranges.
Teacher: What shape is this?	I like football
Student: It's a circle.	

Table 2.1 *Useful Patterns and Expressions for Speaking in Class*

Teen learners

Teenagers are beginning to face an age of transition, confusion, and changing bodies and minds. They use more conscious learning in explaining grammatical rules. Most of them are learning because they have to learn.

Therefore they are reluctant to invest effort.

Demanding points in teaching teenagers
- They have difficult period of life since they are unsure about themselves and their feelings.
- They have rising and falling interest and emotions. Therefore, implementing some techniques and activities are needed.
- They get bored quickly and their level of motivation is low.
- They hate discipline.
- They are always fed up.

Specific ideas in teenage classes
- Avoid using childish materials for teenagers.
- Use group work when whole-class work doesn't seem to be working.
- Avoid using activities that cause embarrassment.
- Choose reading and listening activities from up-to-date sources.
- Ask learners to bring in materials based on their interest.
- Be trustful. Try to say what you really think about things.
- Don't get bothered when a strong argument is presented.
- De-emphasize competition between classmates.

Adult learners
- Adults can handle abstract rules and concepts.
- Adults have longer attention spans on materials in which they are not interested.
- Adults can use their multiple senses in learning.
- Adults often bring their general self-confidence into a classroom.
- Adults have developed abstract thinking ability to understand segments of language.

Adults' classroom management
- Avoid making discipline in adult classes in the same way as children.
- Give students as many opportunities as possible to have choices in cooperative learning.
- Avoid treating them like children by calling them "kids" and talking down to them.

Learning how to learn

It is an important point for learners to be taught the needed skills in order to learn how to learn effectively. Teachers should help learners whatever age they are to learn the following purposeful and goal-oriented learning strategies:

- Repeating new words over and over
- Listening carefully to distinguish words
- Making hypotheses about rules
- Trying out the hypotheses
- Testing learning to remember words
- Guessing the meaning of unfamiliar words
- Applying language rules to make new sentences
- Practicing skills and components of language in head

Introducing learning strategies in case of facing an unfamiliar task

- **Asking question:** considering the parameters of the task
- **Planning:** considering necessary tactics
- **Checking:** considering the evaluation of performance
- **Re-drafting:** considering re-calculation of goals
- **Self-assessment:** considering final results

Teaching learning strategies

Teachers should be aware of the importance of teaching learning strategies to learners. There are different ways to reach the goals. Teachers can name the strategy or explain how it works step by step. Making interviews or questionnaire can be helpful as well. Verbalizing the strategies while teachers are doing the strategy is another way to provide successful experience.

Classroom games
Easy games for little children

Nothing can engage children in learning better than teaching English through playing. Indeed a bored class takes in less than half of what a teacher says and retains none of it. Whereas an interested and involved class, learning through fun English Language games, takes in 100% of the lesson and retains up to 80% of it. Using language games should be one of the most exciting ways to teach English to children. There are a lot of benefits of using games in language-learning. Games make learner-centered classes. They improve communicative competence and make a meaningful context for language use. Learning motivation is increased through games. They decrease learning anxiety and integrate various linguistic skills. Learners' creativity and cooperation in using language can be encouraged. They increase participatory attitudes of the students.

Hands up
It can be used for beginners. E.g. use the flash cards for this game to ask students some questions.
Say "*hands up*" whenever you play this game.

Show me
Teach several alphabets through writing them on the board. Then use flash cards and ask them to show the new letters to you with using flash cards.

Listen and draw
Be a good drawer in children classes. Teach them simple ways to draw some simple objects.

Class mascot
Bring a doll or something like that to class and introduce it to the class and try to use it whenever you want to teach a new language. You can use it for correction. Give a name to it and try to refer to it whenever needed.

Magic box
Bring a box into a class, put some objects even flash cards that the students know and ask them to take out one by one, and ask "*what is this?*"

Elementary games
Typical day
Practices: speaking, present simple
A student describes a typical day with lots of present simple. This can be about his/her typical day, or others.

When you turn
Practices: listening
This game is good for students to learn how to give directions. A student is placed in the middle of the classroom and told to find a word on the board following instructions given by the group.

Animal adventures

Practices: listening, speaking

The teacher tells a story for example about an animal, but repeatedly asks the students to guess what, why, where, what next etc. to challenge students

Example:

Teacher:	A cat did something very naughty. What did it do?
Students:	It ate some cheese.
Teacher:	No.
Students:	It attacked the pet bird.
Teacher:	Yes! That's right! But why?
Students:	Because it was hungry.
Teacher:	No.
Students:	Because it was jealous.

Each time the students "guess" something, there is another question. It is the students who unknowingly invent it.

Verbs and tenses

Practices: getting familiar with English tenses

1. Illustrate known tenses with tense clue words, for example:

    Habit/truth = present simple

    Now = present continuous

    Experience = present perfect

    Plan = going to

2. Select a range of verbs.

3. Divide the class into teams.

4. Give the same verb and tense clue word to each team.

The idea is for each team to make the longest and the best constructed sentence. Count up the words from each team's sentence and score on the board.

Odd-one-out

Practices: vocabulary, speaking

Make a list of four or five words on the board, all but one of which has something in common. Ask the students to find the "odd-one-out".

Ring-a-word

Practices: almost anything

This classic classroom game is guaranteed to wake up the doziest class. It can be used for anything from learning the alphabet to revising irregular verbs.

There are many variations dependent only on the teacher's imagination. The basic idea is that the teacher covers the board randomly with words or letters. One team is given a blue white board marker. The other team is given a red marker. The teams line up on either side of the board with the front students holding the markers. The teacher calls out a letter and the front students try to locate it and draw a ring round it. Change students every call or every three calls etc. The team with the most number of rings at the end wins. Some possible topics (can be mixed) are:

- alphabet
- numbers
- dates
- times
- irregular verbs (e.g. write "v1" and call out "v2" or vice versa)
- prepositions

What am I wearing?
Practices: identify clothes, styles, colors, shapes
Before class draw a circle on the board with four air bubbles coming from it and in each write summer, winter, spring and autumn. Have a discussion about students' favorite clothes and fashions.

Team game
Practices: writing
One student from each team goes to the board and the teacher describes a garment. The winner is the first student to write the correct word with correct spelling.

Intermediate games

Anecdote
Practices: listening, speaking
Each student thinks of a true personal anecdote, something that actually happened in the past. He/she then starts to recount the anecdote but stops after a while and asks the others to guess the end.

Clap
Practices: listening, speaking
The teacher starts telling a story. After a few sentences, the teacher claps his/her hands and asks a student to continue the story. After a few more sentences, the teacher claps his/her hands again and asks another student to continue. Repeat as necessary.

Double jeopardy

Practices: making questions

Teacher or somebody gives an answer, for example a place, a date, a person, a reason etc.

The others try to find the question. E.g.

Answer: *Mont Blanc*

Question: *What is the highest mountain in Europe?*

How?

Practices: speaking, the imperative

Students give mini presentations on "how to do something".

Some sample topics:

- how to start a car
- how to use a photocopier
- how to make a cup of tea
- how to make an omelet
- how to change a tire
- how to change baby's nappy
- how to make a telephone call
- how to play golf

This can be more or less complicated, as the teacher wishes. It can, for example, be a 2-minute delivery with no visual aids, or a 15-minute delivery with handouts followed by questions.

Lion tamer

Practices: yes/no questions

The teacher prepares stickers with a **profession** on each one. The stickers are affixed to students' **foreheads**. Students try to discover their own profession by asking **yes/no** questions (do I work at night? am I rich? do I wear a uniform?) in turn. It works best in small groups.

Secret word

Practices: speaking, questions

Student A leaves the room. The other students choose a secret word. They then ask Student A to return and ask his/her questions to elicit the secret word. Student A must reply fully to all questions without saying the secret word (which, of course, she doesn't know). She loses by saying it.

Improvisations

Practices: speaking

The following ideas are not role-plays or simulations (although many of them can be adapted as such). The objective here is total spontaneity and improvisation. Students have no time to prepare. Their roles and situations are given to them on the spot and they have to react immediately. Generally, the less details that are given to students, the better it is. This allows students to use their own imaginations to construct situations and ensures richer dynamics.

Guess what

Practices: listening, spelling

One member of the class leaves the room and is called back in, after one or two minutes. She is informed that the teacher has told the other students something rather confidential about him/ her. His/ Her task is to discover what the teacher has revealed by asking yes/no questions such as: *Is it about my family? Is it in the classroom?*

Reading comprehension

Practices: reading

Before the students start reading a text in class, show the title and ask them to give the words they believe might appear in the text (the title should help students to guess what the text will be about). After that the words are written on the board. Then the students should compose their own stories based on the title given by the teacher and the vocabulary list on the board and read their text.

Distracters

Practices: almost anything

Select a student who has a good command of the language and ask him/her to sit at the front of the class. Give him/her a sheet of paper with a simple task to do (e.g. a calculation, copying a short paragraph from a textbook, etc.). Tell the class that their role is to impede the student from doing the task by keeping on asking questions. The selected student should stop the activity to answer the questions. You can set a time limit for the student to complete the task in spite of distraction.

Upper intermediate and advanced games

Vacation fun

Practices: sharing information/giving directions

Ask your advanced adult ESL class to make a project about how they managed summer activities. Limit it to a place that is a day trip or a local activity to include everyone. They orally

- share the information (e.g. "My children love the museum.")
- answer questions about the information. (e.g. "Which museum", "the one on Fifth Avenue". After sharing their suggestions they decided to:
  1. Add a photo, postcard or brochure.
  2. Add some personal comments ("The best time is in the morning when it's not crowded.").
  3. Re-do the bulletin board to display their mini-posters.
  4. Provide a place for feedback if others visited the same place.

At the end of the summer they plan to do a survey and write a little article for the school news about the favorite vacation spot. Also, send their posters and feedback to each location's PR office.

How to use more English in the classroom

The best textbooks, teaching materials, syllabi, and even authentic exposure to English will ultimately fail, however, if the ordinary classroom English teachers do not model and use English communicatively, meaningfully, and purposefully in their classrooms. The regular English teachers are the most important people in the English educational settings to encourage students to attempt to communicate through using real English by integrating all language components, skill, and strategies.

Some easy ways to use more English in class

Always use English when opening and closing the class: students will understand the basic idea if you use it at the beginning of every class.

Teach your student "Classroom English": teach your students classroom expressions appropriate for their levels; for example, *I don't know, I don't understand, Once again please, Just a minute, What's a ... in L1 (English)?, Pardon me,* etc. Be sure they understand how to say and use the expressions you expect them to know. You can give them a small handout with the expressions you would like them to use and have them paste it in the back of their notebooks for easy reference.

Use handouts for simple English instructions: use English for very simple instructions such as *Please write -*, *Answer the following questions*, *English only, please*, etc. Read the instructions to the students and explain the instructions by modeling what you want them to do.

Always get the students to write their names using the Roman alphabet: as soon as the students learn to write the letters, insist that they should use them to write their names. Remember this is English class. Getting used to how your own name looks and sounds in a foreign language is a part of personalizing your knowledge of the language.

Teach grammar in English too: for novice teachers, it may seem like an impossible task to teach grammar in English. But it can be done easily. Start with what the students know with providing more and more examples.

Try to use only one or two expressions for the same activity: by limiting the number of classroom expressions the teacher uses, the students will learn the expressions faster.

Have confidence in your own ability: this is essential. The students need a model of a confident ESL speaker to inspire confidence in themselves.

Correct but don't criticize your students: if you want your students to experiment, guess, and practice, you should encourage these behaviors. Let the students know you are pleased that they are trying-even if what they say is incorrect. When they make a mistake, praise them for answering and then ask them to try again

Challenge your students and yourself: try getting through a whole class using as much English as you can. While challenging yourself to speak English completely, encourage students to do that as well.

Implementing these ideas

The suggestions above may be simple and easy, but remember that they aren't a quick fix. If you want them to work, you need to commit yourself to English communication in your classroom, not to the strategies themselves.

Classroom English for teachers

For non-native English teachers who are worried about using non-grammatical or non-idiomatic expressions while teaching, here's a list of classroom expressions based on American English.

Greetings
- *Hello.*

- *Good afternoon (class/ everyone).*
- *Goodbye.*
- *See you tomorrow/ next week/ Friday.*
- *That's all for today.*

Transitions

- *First (of all)...?*
- *Next...*
- *For example...*
- *Now let's ...*
- *After that...*

Directions

- *Check your/ your partner's answers.*
- *Close your books/ notebooks.*
- *Come to the board.*
- *Here is/ are your homework/ tests.*
- *Listen carefully.*
- *Look at page/ part/ number....*
- *Open your (text) books/ notebooks (to page... / chapter ... / section...).*
- *Pass your notebooks/ tests/ papers/ homework to me.*
- *Practice ....*
- *Put your pen/ papers/ books/ everything/ ... away/ in your desks/ in your bags.*
- *Read page ... (aloud).*
- *Repeat after me. / Repeat... again.*
- *Sit down / Be seated.*
- *Stand up.*
- *Take one (handout/ test/ copy/ ...).*
- *Take out your pen/ pencil/ notebook/ textbook/ homework ....*
- *Translate this into English/ L1.*
- *Turn to page....*
- *Write the answer on the board/ in you notebooks.*

(Please can be used with the above expressions.)

Questions:

- *Can you tell me (...)?*
- *Do you have any questions?*

- *Do you know what I mean?*
- *Do you understand?*
- *What's … in English? / What does it/ …mean in English?*
- *What's … in L1? / What does it/ … mean in L1?*
- *What's the answer?*
- *Who can tell me (…)?*
- *Who has a question (about…)?*
- *Who knows (…)?*
- *Who knows (the answer)?*
- *Who will volunteer (to…)? /Who will do it?*
- *Who's absent today?*
- *Will you volunteer (to…)? / Will you do it?*

Disciplinary Expressions:

- *Be quiet / Stop talking.*
- *Calm down.*
- *Don't do that.*
- *Listen (to me).*
- *Look (at me).*
- *Put that/ … away.*
- *Stop that/ Stop it.*

(*Please* can be used with the above expressions—but if the teacher is very angry or frustrated she or he probably wouldn't use it.)

- *Are you listening?*
- *Are you paying attention?*
- *What are you doing?*

Classroom English for Students

Students need to learn some expressions if they are to communicate in English in the class. Naturally, teachers should help them with pronunciation, meaning, and usage.

- *(Are you speaking to) me?*
- *Again, please.*
- *Pardon me!*
- *Excuse me?*
- *How do you say this word?*

- *I didn't hear you.*
- *I don't know.*
- *I don't understand. (Huh?)*
- *I think....*
- *I'm thinking.*
- *Just a minute, please.*
- *More slowly, please.*
- *Ms. .../ Mr.... Please help me*
- *That's easy/ difficult/ strange.*
- *What does ...mean?*
- *What's ... in English?*
- *What's ... in L1?*

Definition and functions of task

Defining *"Task"* is a controversial issue based on its *scope*, its *perspective*, its *authenticity*, its required *skills* to perform, its required *psychological processes*, and its *outcome*. Its scope contains eliciting language use to learn a language. The perspective of the task refers to whether a task is considered from the task designers' point of view or the participants'. Authenticity concerns about the need of correspondence to some real world activity. Required skills should explicitly be addressed in performing a task. There are a lot of cognitive processes such as comprehending, manipulating, producing, interacting, selecting, reasoning, or sequencing information that are needed to get learners involved in the task. Outcome of the task refers to what the participants reach when they have completed the task.

Needed task elements

- **Input data:** materials that learners work on
- **Activities:** what learners do with the input
- **Objectives:** the aims of activities
- **Teachers' roles:** the teachers' personalities and their ways of teaching
- **Students' roles:** the students' personalities and their active roles in learning
- **Setting of learning**: foreign language settings and/or second language settings

Main features of tasks

- They should contain plans for learner activity.
- They generally focus on meaning at first.
- They address real-world language use.
- They should cover all language skills.
- They include cognitive processes.
- They should have communicative outcome.
- They should be relevant to students' needs.
- They should be motivating.
- They should be challenging.

Tasks and language teaching

Tasks are used to make language teaching more communicative and effective. They develop learners' abilities to communicate in real world through interactional (using language to maintain contact) and transactional (using language to exchange information) functions. Task-based language teaching includes a thorough classification of communicative activities that can emphasize on students' full potential for growth.

Task classification

- **Closed task** requires learners to make a single or correct solution.
- **Open task** involves learners with unpreditermined solution.
- **Consciousness-raising task** makes learners aware of language points to be able to think about and communicate through language.
- **Convergent task** makes learners agree to a solution to an issue.
- **Divergent task** makes learners defend their different viewpoints on an issue.
- **Focused task** is made to elicit students' incidental attention to particular linguistic forms while processing input or output.
- **Unfocused task** is made to improve language comprehension and production in order to communicate.
- **Information gap task** needs one participant with no information and the others with information to exchange information to complete the task.
- **Opinion-gap task** causes exchanging information among learners who have different information to complete the task.

71

- **Reasoning-gap task** requires learners to engage in deducing new facts by reasoning.
- **Jigsaw task** needs dividing the input material between two or more participants. One participant is not sufficient to complete the task.
- **Reciprocal task** involves information being exchanged between two or more participants.
- **Structured task** leads using a ready-made schema for completing the task.
- **Target task** is similar to real world situation.

Using the board

One resource that every teacher has is a board, whether it is a small board, a wide chalk, a pen board or an interactive computer board. Here are some suggestions to use the board effectively. At the beginning of the lesson, draw a few dividing lines on the board, e.g. to form three working areas, like this:

Review section	Drawing	Vocabulary and grammar

Figure 2.1 *How to Manage the Board*

Teachers should write different things in each section
- A vocabulary column for new words, expressions, and grammatical points.
- A review section to remind students of the previous lesson.
- A place to draw pictures to increase learning while he/she is telling a story or teaching the reading.

Here are a few board thoughts
- Avoid long teacher-writing times. In this case students just watch and wait. Write on the board in a way that your body doesn't block everyone from seeing.
- Whenever possible, make opportunities to write things up on the board while students are working on other activities, so that you are ready when they finish.

Tools/technologies, techniques, and activities

In recent years, the use of aids, tools, techniques, and activities has increasingly become a common feature of the classroom. Here is a range of ideas to try out in class.

Flashcards

Flashcards include pictures, diagrams, words, etc. Typically, they are something you can hold up while standing in front of the whole class. Here are a few typical uses:

- To show the meaning of a lexical item
- To illustrate presentations of language
- To tell a story
- To remind students specific grammatical points
- To prompt guessing games, defining games, and describing games

Picture stories

Pictures and picture stories can be in a book or handout. Teachers approach these materials in a variety of ways for writing, speaking and listening exercises. Through picture stories teachers can make use of two approaches.

1. Accuracy to fluency
- Introduce the topic.
- Focus on interesting or essential lexis, grammar, or function.
- Look at the pictures and discuss based on focused language.
- Tell the story.
- Encourage writing exercise.

2. Fluency to accuracy
- Introduce the topic.
- Look at the picture and discuss.
- Tell the story.
- Focus on interesting or essential lexis, grammar or function
- Tell the story ignoring students' grammatical mistakes to encourage them to speak freely.
- Encourage writing exercise.

Storytelling

Teacher talking time (TTT) is a bad thing, and it should be cut down.

Storytelling is a useful activity for the end of a lesson to provide a change of mood. It should be like mother reading to her children at bedtime not as a chance for teachers to talk and talk.

Basic stages in storytelling are

- mentally preparing your story beforehand
- giving clear instructions along the lines
- telling your story
- letting students talk about it when it's over
- leaving it and going to another activity

Songs and music

Many course books nowadays include songs that focus on grammatical or functional items. For the last two decades, EFL (English as a Foreign Language) methodology has been actively considering the possibility of using music and songs in class. Teachers can

- practice the **rhythm, stress and the intonation patterns** of the English language.
- teach **vocabulary**, especially in the vocabulary reinforcement stage.
- teach **grammar**. In this respect songs are especially favored by teachers while investigating the use of the tenses.
- teach **speaking**. For this purpose, songs and mainly their lyrics are employed as a stimulus for class discussions.
- teach **listening comprehension**.
- develop **writing skills**. For this purpose a song can be used in a variety of ways--for example, speculating what could happen to the characters in the future, writing a letter to the main character, etc.

Ideas for using songs in class

- **Gapped text:** give students the lyrics with certain words blanked out.
- **Song jumble:** cut the lyrics up into separate lines. Make students work out the original order.
- **Reading or listening comprehension:** ask some comprehension questions.
- **Dictation:** ask students to write all the song.

- **Listen and discuss:** ask the subject of the song and make an interesting discussion.
- **Sing along:** ask eager students to sing the song chorally. It makes students fresh to start a new activity.

Ideas for using music in class

- Set the mood at the start of the lesson.
- Help students relax.
- Use it simply for pleasure or as a break.

Fillers

Most teachers think they need a collection of fillers, i.e. things to do when they have finished materials because the main activity went much faster than expected. Revision dictation, yes / no questions, and games are considered as fillers.

Dictionaries

Teachers have suggested that students buy and use a good printed dictionary. But as digital materials improve, some of the advice teachers give may need to change. Any students with Internet access can make use of good free dictionaries online. Mobile phone can download dictionary apps. The existence of thesaurus tools within dictionaries can be also very useful.

Limitations of using bilingual dictionaries for learners

- It is not easy to work out which of a number of different translations can be the correct one; there is no information to help learners distinguish between entries.
- They don't tell learners more than the part of speech.
- There are usually no examples of items being used in sentences.
- Collocations are rarely mentioned.
- Pronunciation information tends to be idiosyncratic.

Teachers' use of dictionary in class activities

- Finding the number of the syllables in a word and learning the place of a word stress
- Interpreting definitions
- Choosing the word that best expresses the meanings you want
- Distinguishing between different meanings of the same word

- Selecting the correct grammatical form of a word and finding the plural of a word
- Making use of collocations
- Finding idiomatic expressions
- Checking the correct spelling of a word

The following activities work on different dictionary skills.

- **Guessing spelling:** write out some words with missing letters. Make pupils guess the missing letters.
- **Which words:** provide gapped sentences and a choice of two or more. Get the students to guess the answer through using their dictionaries to decide the best choice.
- **Finding the stress:** write up words. Ask students to predict the main stress.
- **Dictionary race:** set a number of above activities and have students work through them within a relatively tight time limit.
- **Upgrading:** ask students to go through a written task and find a better way of saying by using dictionary.
- **Alongside reading:** avoid making readers look up every word. Make an agreement on a set of words which the students are allowed to look up.
- **Explore:** help students use dictionary entries to look around words they know already to enrich what they can do with familiar items such as collocations.

Timelines

They are teaching aids that can be used to help explain how different verb tenses are used. They are a visual representation of the passage of time. This is an empty timeline:

Past	Now	Future

Poetry and drama

Language teaching can be dull but poetry stimulates and wakes learners up to see things in a new way, hear things in new ways, think of things in new ways. There are some drama activities found in English language classes

- Playing scripts
- Drama games
- Guided improvisation or prepared improvised drama
- Role play
- Stimulation

Films

They are classic lazy teachers who use video materials once in a while. But it is important that we find ways to exploit them in useful ways to increase learning. Like all language skill teaching, watching films should be based on three stages. **Pre-watching** making students ready to guess what is going to be played, **watching** considering the content of the film, and **post-watching** focusing on comprehension by asking students to summarize what they have already watched, asking some comprehension questions, and discussing the film.

Technologies in class

Technologies have begun to change the way that English is learned in the classroom. In a world where we increasingly see laptops, tablet computers, or mobile phones as the technology of choice, learning English through these devices gains credibility. These digital tools are, of course, central in the establishment of the field of computer assisted language learning (CALL), but are also increasingly a core part of English language teaching (ELT) in general. It is important to make sure that the technologies that we have available are used effectively. Technology here means using internet, video conferencing (Polycom) with whiteboard facility, and PowerPoint.

Teaching culture

Culture permeates every aspect of our beings. Before getting started, it's a good idea that the teacher gives a cultural background in his/her class. Language teachers must be interested in the study of culture to make enthusiasm and better learning. Teaching a language without its culture is just teaching meaningless symbols to such extent that the students cannot be able to compare the cultural values of two societies.

Using video materials, newspapers, magazines, are good sources of bringing culture to the class. The teacher can introduce culture through reciting history and literature of a country. As a general rule, take advantage of any opportunity to talk about culture with open mind.

If proper attention is paid to explaining the cultural differences when you teach a new language, the students will come to realize that cultures are different and not superior or inferior.

Current research findings

For different learners effective classroom strategies have traditionally contained use of songs, rhymes, films, and traditional stories with repeated language structures. The internet can be a rich source of authentic oral models via recorded songs, talking electronic books, podcasts and video clips that help learners with pronunciation as well as acquisition and reinforcement of new vocabulary. These tools can also help teachers encourage students who don't feel confident with their own language skills. Technology also provides learners with the opportunity to record themselves to play back at a later time. Learners report that the ability to listen and play back recordings helps identification of grammatical errors and inaccuracy in pronunciation, and encouraging self-improvement.

Conclusion

English teachers should provide learners with necessary words, phrases, and sentences to be able to cope with communication in English from the first step of learning English. Characteristics of different learners, techniques for teaching English to them, learning how to learn, and teaching learning strategies have been discussed.

Games can be effective tools in English classes. A number of factors should be considered in using games. In terms of choosing games, teachers should be aware of students' learning styles. This is in order to provide games that best suit students. Some students may prefer to work alone than in group. As a result, they may not take any parts in group work assigned to them. In addition, different games serve different purposes, so when designing a teaching plan, teachers should specify in which stage games would be employed.

In recent years a debate has developed over which approaches to structuring and planning and implementing lessons are more effective and useful. Teachers should be familiar with those tasks that work best for learning and teaching. There are different kinds of tasks to be used in English to increase the process of learning. Language system should be acquired through the process of interacting, negotiating, and communicating meaningfully in purposeful tasks.

These days, English classrooms are extremely diverse. There are many teachers who ignore the diversity of the students they teach. There are many types of different learner groups, such as children, young learners, and adults. Students all come from different backgrounds, have different interests and have different learning preference that they are used to. It is important to use the best methods of teaching based on different student population to be an effective teacher.

CHAPTER THREE

The Practical Teacher
"The best teachers teach from the heart, not from the book."
Anonymous

Introduction

Teaching-learning is a lifelong process. A teacher should be a student as well. Good teachers are not born but they are made. All non-native teachers face difficulty teaching vocabulary and grammar. They need hard training to stand up with confidence to enter the teaching profession. Teachers will become confident by and by. Loving teaching is the best step to succeed. A good teacher is the one who analyses beforehand what he/she wants to convey to his/her learners; in fact an everlasting training and self- development may highly be needed to achieve flexibility and thus confidence.

Characteristics of a good teacher
There are many distinct characteristics of a good teacher. A good teacher

- is an entertainer in a positive sense, not a negative one.
- is somebody who has an affinity to the students.
- is someone who generously helps.
- is someone who knows students' names and is a good psychologist and listener.
- avoids being *too* friendly with the students.
- doesn't play with cell phones and doesn't leave the class without reasons.
- is always punctual.
- should tolerate the quiet students and control the more talkative ones.
- should love his/her job. If he/she really enjoys it, that'll make the lessons more interesting.
- should be sharp and a good manager to correct students without offending them.
- should make lessons interesting and entertaining so that students don't fall asleep
- is energetic, humorous, and charismatic.

- is not domineering but knows how to control students tactfully.
- is knowledgeable about language and other fields.
- doesn't hide his/her own personality.
- is well-dressed and polite.
- involves students in leaning. *"Tell me, I forget. Teach me, I remember. Involve me, I learn."*

Teachers are more than a book, a classroom, and some students. A teacher has multidimensional roles in every educational setting. Some teachers make very strong feeling of dislike for students.

Hated teachers

They are bad tempered and unsmiling. Mostly they are dictator like. Learners get bored with their sticking to one point for a long time. They cause fear and tension in class. Generally they dislike teaching so overload students with homework. They raise the voice and look nervous.

Introductory activities after entering the class

Teachers can do the following activities at the beginnings of all sessions:

- Put on smile as you enter the class.
- Break the ice to reduce tension.
- Call the roll.
- Bring joy to your classroom.
- Check the homework.
- Review the previous units; ask some Yes/No, Wh- questions, or the summary of the previous lesson.

Tips for teaching on the first day of class

Arrive in time: be sure you know where the classroom is. Talk with students before class starts. Interaction makes them willing to participate in class. Make sure that the room is ready and equipped.

Introduce yourself first: write your name and the course title on the board and share contact information.

Clarify the course organization, requirements, major assignments, and policies: students feel more comfortable if you are organized and prepared. Have a well-written, detailed syllabus ready to hand out. Talk about exams, papers, books to be covered, policies, academic integrity, grades, etc.

Describe your expectations for class participation: give students a sense of your teaching style and your expectations for their involvement. If attendance and class participation are necessary, make that clear to the students, as well as how you grade them.

Spark off interest in the course material: leave students interested in learning the material. Present your vision, or overview, of the course. Relate the course topic to current applications or issues. Communicate the importance of the course that you are starting.

"Build a sense of community" and make a positive tone: if you "build a sense of community," students will perform better because they feel connected to the class and to the instructor. Learn your students' names. Students appreciate fair and objective instructors who show willingness to work in a course.

Plan to use at least one of your teaching methods: prepare a brief lecture or a focused discussion that demonstrates to students at least one of the methods you use. It is important to do so *on the first day*.

Welcome students' questions: try to answer the questions that students bring into the class.

Teachers and students should talk in class

- It is important to get students to talk by using the language they have learned.
- Students are the people who need practice in talking so the more they talk, the more they receive practice in language learning.
- Students should be exposed to language to talk more.
- *Comprehensible input* is an important feature in language acquisition and the first and the best input is teachers' talking.

How should teachers talk to students?

- Use more exaggerated tones of voice.
- Speak with less complex grammatical structures.
- Use restricted vocabulary.
- Use more body language and physical movement.
- Adapt the language to the level of the students (*level adaptation*).
- Show happiness and sadness in playing the roles.
- Concentrate the focus on students' comprehension.
- Learn about how to talk to students.

What should the novice teachers ask before giving instruction?

- What is the information I am trying to convey?
- What must the students know if they are to complete the activity successfully?
- Which information do they need first?
- Which should come next?

The art of teachers questioning

Why should teachers ask questions?

- To **involve** students in the lesson.
- To increase **motivation** or interest.
- To **evaluate** students' preparation.
- To check on **completion of work.**
- To develop **critical thinking** skills.
- To **review** previous lessons.
- To nurture **insights**.
- To **assess** achievement or mastery of goals and objectives.
- To stimulate **independent learning**.

Strategies in asking questions

1. Write out some questions when planning the lesson.
   - Include notes of when you will pause to ask and answer questions.
   - Use both preplanned and emerging questions.
2. Cue students before asking the question. You should not single out students in advance. First ask the question and then call a student. This is done to involve all students.
   - Call on a specific student.
   - Ask students to raise their hands.
   - Ask students to shout out the answer.
   - Ask all students to think of an answer before asking the question.
3. Avoid asking "leading questions". Follow a "yes-or-no" question with an additional question.
4. Avoid questions with only one acceptable answer.
5. Phrase questions carefully, concisely, and clearly.
6. Call on a variety of students. Give every student equal opportunity to take

part

How to ask questions tactfully
Try keeping students on their toes

1. Use questions to identify **learning objectives** to follow up self-study.
2. Ask questions that are at the **appropriate level** for each student.
3. Ask questions that **elicit positive or correct responses**.
4. Use **differentiating** questions from the more difficult and complex part of the particular topic at hand to the less.
5. Encourage **students to ask** questions.

How to respond to answers more effectively

1. Use sufficient wait time.
2. Do not interrupt students' answers.
3. Show that you are interested in students' answers, whether right or wrong.
4. If a student gives an incorrect or weak answer ask the student a follow-up question that will lead that student to the correct answer.
5. Develop responses that keep students thinking.

Asking questions using Bloom's educational Taxonomy
Six levels of complexity

1. Knowledge: memorizing information
2. Comprehension: rephrasing
3. Application: problem solving
4. Analysis: comparing and contrasting
5. Synthesis: composing
6. Evaluation: making decision

- **Use Lower-order thinking:** (fact, closed, direct, recall, and knowledge questions) to assess students' knowledge and comprehension
- **Use Higher-order thinking:** (open-ended, interpretive, evaluative, inquiry, inferential, and synthesis questions) to assess students' abilities to apply, analyze, synthesize, and evaluate

Why should teachers ask higher level questions?
- Make students think critically to avoid repeating literal information.

- Develop positive self-concept to make students active knowledge producers rather than passive knowledge consumers.
- Make students comprehend what the author is really trying to say to increase students' inference ability.
- Develop self-questioning to make active learners.

Some kinds of questions

1. **Staged questioning:** to boost level of challenge. E.g. *what is this? when do you use it? how does it work?*

2. **Olympic challenge questioning:** to make competition. E.g. *who would like to get "Gold" and who would like to answer the Gold question?*

3. **Quality control questioning**: to improve debating ability. E.g. *who is for this topic? who is against this topic? who has a different answer?*

4. **Secondary questioning**: to ask students to explain an answer (either their own or that of another student) in more detail

5. **Information getting questioning:** to ask students to *"Go on..."*

6. **Challenging questioning:** instead of *"How many examples of similes/metaphors can you find?"* try; *"There are n number of examples of similes/metaphors – can you find them all?"*

7. **Opinion based questioning:** to make less threatening opinion based/discussion answers. *"Do you believe that...?"*

8. **Limited maximum/minimum answering:** to make students answer in not more/fewer than 15 words.

9. **Mixed ability questioning:** to improve individuals' self-esteem rapidly.
   - working one to one
   - targeting whole class questions at one student

10. **With Silent teachers:** to make students run the lesson by asking questions about a topic.

Teachers' error correction

When a second language learner develops his/her language system, he/she makes errors. As in first language learning, some of these errors are "lapses", or "slips of tongue" due to physical or psychological reasons. Some on the other hand occur regularly and show the misunderstanding of the second language system.

Errors are the best signs of learning.

In communicative language teaching **errors are tolerated during**

fluency-based activities. The teacher may note errors during fluency activities and return to them later with an accuracy- based activity. **No on the spot error correction** is suggested; *(Direct correction is more effective but it can be demotivating)* the correction may be made as the following stages:

1- Self correction

2- Peer correction

3-Teacher correction

Two kinds of errors:

- **Global errors:** they interrupt communication (e.g., serious pronunciation or vocabulary errors).
- **Local errors:** they do not interrupt communication.

Distinction between error and mistake

- **Error** (lapse in knowledge): lapse is consistent (e.g., constantly says "he go, want...")
- **Mistake** (lapse in performance): lapse is occasional (e.g., occasionally says "he go or he goes")

Types of corrective feedback

Lyster and Ranata (1996) identified seven types of feedback given by the teachers:

Explicit correction: teachers give correct form.

Recast: teachers reformulate student's attempt.

Clarification request: teachers ask a follow-up question.

Metalinguistic feedback: teachers talk about the error, perhaps using the grammatical language.

Elicitation: teachers stop and ask the student or another student to correct the form.

Repetition: teachers sometimes repeat the error with highlighting by intonation.

Multiple: teachers use a mixture of the above. In this study the most popular feedback strategy is recasting, to correct student's utterance and reformulate it.

How to indicate that an error has been made

- Telling that there is an error
- Using facial expression
- Using gestures

- Using finger correction
- Repeating the sentence up to error
- Echoing the sentence with changing intonation or stress
- Asking questions
- Writing the wrong sentence on the board
- Exploit fun in the error

The type of classroom climate is considered to be the best facilitating when learning is described as purposeful, task-oriented, relaxed, warm, and supportive process and has a sense of order.

Teachers' roles in autonomous learning

The teacher as a facilitator, resource and counselor is able to state a condition that the learner, based on his/her autonomy, takes charge of learning, sets realistic goals, uses learning strategies, and evaluates learning process.

Teachers' roles in making students autonomous learners

- Make students take charge of their own learning.
- Make them set realistic goals and plan programs of work.
- Make them use learning strategies effectively and develop strategies for coping with new situations.
- Make them create and make good use of study environment.
- Make them evaluate and assess their own learning process.
- Ask before telling.
- Provide everyone with a chance to engage in learning.
- Stretch students' minds with open and relevant questions.
- Pose thinking questions.
- Raise awareness.
- Pose the motivational and inspirational questions.
- Use questions to develop interest in a topic.

Increasing the learner's self-confidence

Providing comfortable classroom with less anxiety and sufficient word of encouragement while the students are asked to do interesting tasks and experience success can be an important factor to develop students' competence which has direct influence on increasing learners' self-confidence.

Teachers' interpersonal skills

Teachers need to familiarize themselves with communication skills and the importance of their tone, volume, rhythm, and emotions while dealing with students. Effective body language, empathy, and good sense of humor create an appropriate atmosphere for learners.

- **Clearly communicate your expectations:** talk about those facts, ideas, events, and points of view that, students will understand throughout the course.
- **Self-disclosure:** share a relevant story of your own experiences in similar situations.
- **Understand and then be understood:** understand the problem from students' points of view.

Teachers' beliefs

It is believed that teachers are influenced by their beliefs. Teachers' beliefs about learning, learners, and teaching profession will affect everything that they do in the classroom. Beliefs about learners range from *registrars* who do not want to learn but only do because they are made to, *receptacles* that will be filled with knowledge, *raw materials*, to be molded into a fine work of art, *clients* who think of teachers as an advisor, *partners* who like to negotiate, and *Explorers* who make decisions upon their goals. Good teachers, consider students as explorers and help them reach their goals in learning.

Teachers' encouragement

Teachers can enhance the strength of learning experiences if they provide their students with the followings

- A sense of capability
- A sense of self-control
- An ability of goal-setting
- An ability of coping with challenges
- An awareness of change
- A positive belief in outcomes
- An intention of being sharing and caring
- A recognition of individuality
- A sense of belongings to the class

Teacher-student rapport

Rapport means increasing similarities and decreasing differences. It is a close agreement between the teacher and his /her students. It causes motivation since it is the relationship that the students have with the teachers. The following ideas suggest improving teacher-student rapport

- Teachers should be friendly and sympathetic to their students.
- Teachers should use some strategies to remember students' names.
- Teachers should listen to students individually and show that they are interested in what they say.
- Teachers who respect students do their best in teaching.
- Working hard on lesson plans along with good teaching methods is also the way to establish rapport in the class.
- To be modest and honest can be considered as main characteristics to build up a good relationship between teachers and students.

Teachers' awareness of multiple intelligences

Teachers should plan projects, lessons, and assessments around the multiple intelligences (*MI*) theory. Howard Gardner states that all human beings have multiple intelligences. These multiple intelligences can be encouraged, or discouraged. He believes each individual has nine intelligences. Like intelligence itself, the adaptations make infinite variety.

Multiple Intelligences

Visual-spatial intelligence refers to using physical space, tools, models, graphics, charts, photographs, drawings, modeling, video, videoconferencing, television, multimedia, texts.

Bodily-kinesthetic intelligence refers to the use of the body effectively like movement, touching, communicating well through body language

Musical intelligence refers to sensitivity to rhythm and sound, and music.

Interpersonal intelligence refers to interacting with others, making friends, empathy for others, group activities, seminars, and dialogues.

Intrapersonal intelligence refers to understanding one's own interests, and goals through independent study and introspection, creative materials, and diaries.

Linguistic intelligence refers to using words effectively through reading, playing word games, making up poetry or stories.

Logical-mathematical intelligence refers to reasoning, calculating, thinking conceptually, abstractly through solving puzzles, asking cosmic questions, logic games, investigations, and mysteries.

Existential intelligence refers to sensitivity and capacity to manage deep questions about human existence, such as the meaning of life, why do we die, and how did we get here.

Naturalist intelligence refers to ability to recognize and classify plants, animals and other objects in nature

Teachers' development

The first year of teaching has possible initial problems. Here are some practical ideas on how to overcome them.

- Observing other classes
- Sharing techniques and methods
- Developing through reading and further study
- Getting feedback from students
- Discussing with colleagues
- Reflecting your own daily activities

Teachers' knowledge

Teachers need to have professional language knowledge, procedural knowledge, and personal knowledge.

- **Professional knowledge** refers to intellectual discipline, theories, and concepts. It includes knowledge about language, knowledge about language learning, and knowledge about language teaching. Teachers can acquire professional knowledge from training programs, books, journals, and conferences.

- **Procedural knowledge** represents knowing how to manage classroom learning and teaching. It is about making supportive relationships with students, organizing optimal teaching methods, using managerial strategies etc.

- **Personal knowledge** involves teachers' ability to recognize their own identities, beliefs, and values.

Teachers' clothes and look

Teachers are judged by administrators, parents, and students by the way they dress. While some schools permit casual clothes, others impose a code.

Either way, teachers must dress professionally to gain respect from others. Teachers should look exceptional, charismatic, and interesting. Sometimes it is necessary to practice in the mirror and with each other until you can do well on demand without smiling. This look will stop disruptive behavior before it becomes a problem

Teachers' taboos

English teachers should have a fine balance between being themselves and showing respect. They should take active steps to learn about the culture and customs of people and the place of teaching. This includes finding out about the taboo topics and actions that could embarrass, confuse or upset a student. Taboos can be found in words, gestures, topics, social and cultural behavior, body language, and personal space.

It is said, that what is appropriate in a country may be considered rude, insulting or even bad luck in another one. Talking about taboos in general can also be tricky.

Teachers should make sure not to promote generalizations or stereotypes that could upset or insult anyone. General *topics for teachers to avoid* discussing in a multicultural class:

- Religious beliefs
- Racial abuse
- Poverty
- Polygamy
- Political beliefs
- Sexuality
- Historical Conflict

General *actions and gestures for teachers to avoid doing* in a multicultural class:

- Eating or chewing gum in the class
- Embarrassing students
- Holding eye contact for a long period of time
- Pointing
- Standing very close to a student
- Swearing
- Touching students

Teachers' movement

Classrooms are interactive learning environments where negotiated practices become established. In the classroom, teachers' and students' actions, including speech, gestures, expressions, and appearances are used to make communication effectively. Particularly in lectures, the teacher's actions become the means through which the lesson is organized and interaction is structured.

Teachers' needs

Teaching is a challenging profession. All the methods and strategies work only if teachers are supported to meet their needs.

- They need to be supported financially by the government or English Institute principals.
- They need to have comfortable chairs and tables.
- They need to have available markers, dusters, lists of students' names, audio-visual players.
- They need to be respected by principals, parents, and students.
- They need to have breaks between classes.
- The classes shouldn't be overcrowded.
- They shouldn't be forced to take more classes that cause tension and fatigue.

Teachers' task in preparation

Nothing can guarantee a disastrous lesson when the teacher is unprepared. Here are some points:

- **Prepare yourself.**
  a. Decide what you are teaching.
  b. Make sure you have the necessary materials, markers, dusters, books, etc.
  c. Make sure the DVD player is working.
  d. Look at the materials in the students' book on detail.
  e. Have two or three five-minute fillers.
- **Consider that courses and lessons need an overall structure.**
  a. Stop time to time to think about how you are doing in the class.
  b. Consider the fact that language learning is more important than language teaching.
  c. Think about long-term objectives of any course.

    d. Discuss from time to time how the course relates to students' need.

    e. Work in harmony with the author in spite of flexibility.

    f. Adapt supplement, or omit items from the textbook for a particular class.

- **Be creative in using the book.**

    a. Omit practices of a certain type.

    b. Don't criticize the book.

    c. Tell students before you miss out a particular example.

    d. Do not be afraid to change the order of the material presented in the book.

    e. Plan changes in advance

- **Do not prepare too much or too rigidly.**

    a. Make a plan as a general framework.

    b. Look for opportunities to capitalize on the students' interest.

    c. Put the notes somewhere you can see them without inconvenience.

    d. Don't keep the notes a secret.

- **Make concrete preparation.**

    a. Use positive/negative tables to encourage students to think widely and imaginatively, but at the same time concretely.

    b. Use best/worst tables to encourage a wide range of concrete ideas.

- **Never ignore the practical difficulties.**

    a. Be conscious of each and every student as an individual.

    b. Be sure all students hear you.

    c. Be sure all students hear the DVD player.

    d. Be sure all students see your lips during a pronunciation practice.

- **Make a lesson with a beginning, a middle, and an end.**

    a. Begin your class with a short introduction. Provide a short summary of what will happen next time.

Ethics in the classroom

Teachers' work covers many things: one of them is ethics. Ethics is more than just a code of principles and rules. Teachers are engaged in one of the most demanding jobs, educating people; thus teachers need to reflect on the ethics of their activities to ensure that in their work they represent the best example of ethics to those they are morally educating.

Unethical and improper teachers' behaviors

- Increasing grades due to parental pressure without justification
- Spending class time engaging in irrelevant activities
- Failing to keep an accurate record of students' performance
- Rewarding or punishing students based on students' popularity, culture, and ethnicity
- Engaging in a romantic relationship with students
- Refusing to fail students, even when they perform poorly
- Discussing confidential information about a student with others
- Hiring students to do chores
- Making disrespectful comments about a colleague
- Copying and distributing published material without giving credit

Current research findings

The changes that have taken place in educational system have changed the roles of teachers, too. Nowadays teachers provide information and show their students how to tackle them. They can be thought of as facilitators in the learning process. They can choose the teaching materials and make up a syllabus of their own. They need to be an information technology expert, a technician, and photocopy master. The school needs them as individuals, who can make decisions and manage the stress of the changing world of schools.

Conclusion

In this chapter teachers' important characteristics to be adaptable and to be able to do different roles at different stages of teaching have been discussed. Creating good teacher-student rapport has an integral role in teaching. It is mentioned that teachers should be always prepared. Among the skills teachers need to acquire, are the ability to adjust tasks to different learners, to manage time and classes, to provide lessons, and to offer clear teaching techniques.

Teachers need to acquire knowledge of the language system, materials, and classroom equipment. The art of teachers questioning, teachers' error correction, types of corrective feedback in the classroom, teachers' roles in autonomous learning, teachers' roles in increasing the learner's self-confidence, teachers' interpersonal skills, and teachers' beliefs are important to motivate students to participate in English classes to learn English adequately. Other factors such as teachers' encouragement, teacher-student rapport, teachers' awareness of multiple intelligences, teachers' clothes and look, teachers' needs, and teachers' task in preparation based on ethics in the classroom should not be ignored.

CHAPTER FOUR

Syllabus Design, Lesson Planning, and Classroom Management
"If you fail to plan, you plan to fail".   Anonymous

Introduction

yllabus design, lesson planning, and classroom management are of
Sparamount importan   ce   in   the   English   teaching-
learning process. The course that a teacher is going to teach should be
based on some kind of syllabus rules and regulations. Planning is viewed as a
key aspect of a successful lesson as well. While planning, the teacher needs to
make several decisions about activities, objectives, timing, grouping, and other
aspects of the lessons. Classroom management refers to the wide variety of
skills and techniques that teachers use to keep students organized, and
focused. **It** is a term used by teachers to describe the process of ensuring that
classroom lessons run smoothly despite disruptive behavior by some students.

1.   Syllabus design and need analysis

According to Nunan (1988), **Curricula** are concerned with making
general statements about language learning, learning purpose and experience,
evaluation, and the role of teachers and learners. In the curriculum design
process, environment analysis (lists of factors and the effects of these factors
on the design), needs analysis (a realistic list of language and skills about the
present proficiency, future needs and wants of learners), and principles
(deciding on the most essential principles to apply through the whole design
process) should be considered. Evaluation can be used in every aspect of a
course to examine if the course is adequate and where it requires
improvement (Nation & Macalister, 2010). A general curriculum model can be
studied from different perspectives:

Curriculum planning is decision making process considering learners' needs
and purposes; setting goals and objectives; selecting and grading content,
materials, tasks; organizing appropriate learning arrangements and learner
groupings; and evaluation and assessment tools.

Observing in action takes us into the classroom itself, to identify the
advantages and disadvantage of the design.

Evaluation is trying to determine what students had learned and what they
had failed based on what had been planned and what changes should be made
to improve things in future.

Management is looking at the resources available and how they are used.

Syllabus is a subcomponent of curriculum. It is the arrangement of subjects for study over a period of time. Syllabi are more restricted and are based on records of what actually happens at the classroom level as teachers and learners apply a given curriculum to their own situation. *Syllabus design* is being focused on the selection and grading of content, *(what)* while *methodology* is focused on the selection of learning tasks and activities *(How to deal with content)*.

A syllabus aids at teaching and learning of language and contributes to the learners' achievement of communicative competence because it provides teachers and learners with a plan to follow. Some syllabuses focus on specifications of content *(product syllabuses)*; others include guidance on teaching and learning as well as content *(process syllabuses)*. The key issue that has emerged in the development of theory in ELT syllabus design appears to be managing the tensions between content (product) and process (methods of teaching and learning). Nunan (1988) noted that this dichotomy can be inspected either narrowly or broadly. The narrow inspection sees the syllabus design as focusing on the ordering of content. The broad inspection, however, sees syllabus design as considering teaching and learning processes.

Characteristics of a good syllabus

- It consists of content items which are words, structures, and topics, and process items which are tasks and methods.
- Items are based on order. Easier and more essential items come first.
- It has clear objectives generally mentioned in the introduction.
- It may represent a time schedule.
- It may represent a selected methodology or approach.
- It contains a public document to answer the audience.

Different types of syllabi

There are two major types of syllabuses, product-oriented syllabus and process-oriented syllabus. A good and valid syllabus is the one that covers more or less all aspects of both mentioned types. Therefore, proper and appropriate implementation of syllabus in language teaching is undeniable. Without proper implementation of syllabus, on the one hand, desired objectives will be hard to obtain and on the other hand students will suffer from the lack of appropriate syllabus which could fulfill their immediate pedagogical requirements and sharpen their abilities in different areas of language. In this perspective, the characteristics of each syllabus are discussed in a nutshell. All these syllabuses will prove beneficial if carefully implemented.

Any curriculum which doesn't give due consideration to both product and process is defective. Product- and process- oriented syllabuses are seen on a continuum where we should be aiming to take the process into account, but we should also have objectives, that is, we need to state what our learners will be able to do as a result of instruction and what they need to learn.

Product-oriented syllabus

A product-oriented syllabus focuses on things learnt at the end of the learning process (outcomes) rather than the process itself. It can be compared with a process-oriented syllabus, which focuses on the processes of learning. Most syllabi are, and must be, a combination of processes and outcomes. Grammatical, functional and lexical syllabi are product-oriented as they focus on grammatical, functional and lexical outcomes. In the classroom, learners who are working with a product-oriented syllabus can be supported with other approaches and techniques. For example, teachers can incorporate elements of learner training and development from learner-centered syllabi, or use activities from process-oriented syllabi such as task-based learning. The grammatical, situational, lexical, grammatical-lexical, and functional-notional are the examples of product-oriented syllabus.

Grammatical syllabus: a list of grammatical items, such a past tense, superlative of adjectives, relative clauses, generally is used in graded sections based on difficulty or importance. Learners learn grammatical structures in a sequence that represents their complexity, rather than their use in communication, leading to many artificial contexts for practice, and perhaps an inability to change learning to real communication. Organizing learning based on a grammatical syllabus has been criticized but it is still the most common type of syllabus in published materials, mostly because it is the easiest type of syllabus sequencing.

Situational syllabus: real-life contexts of language uses are available in this syllabus. Sections are designed by names of situations or locations such as "eating at a restaurant" to provide realistic situation based on a communicative view of language. **Lexical syllabus:** it is based on vocabulary and lexical units. There are many linguistics issues that can be applied to the lexical syllabus. For example: vocabulary related to topics, word formation (suffixes, morphemes), compound items, connotations, collocations, idioms, and denotations. The similarity or the relationship between lexis and grammar makes difficult to create lexical syllabus because the designers may be confused on selecting an appropriate topic.

Grammatical-lexical syllabus: both structures and lexis are used together.

Functional-notional syllabus: it contains functions that are things you can do with language such as "inviting" and "requesting" and notions things that you can express the language through them. This syllabus is based on learning to express the communicative functions of language and the concepts and ideas to express it.

Process-oriented syllabus

A process-oriented syllabus aims at the skills and processes involved in learning language. It can be compared with a product-oriented syllabus, which focuses on completed acts of communication, the outputs. A process-writing syllabus would focus on the processes writers use to complete their tasks, such as collecting information, organizing ideas, drafting and revising, rather than just the features of the products of writing, such as letters, compositions, notes, reports, etc. In the classroom, working on the writing processes is hard work for learners because it involves thinking, organizing and planning, but it is time well-invested in skills that will enable the learner to become an autonomous writer. One way to apply a process approach to tasks is to provide the language they need on demand as they work, rather than before they start. This can be done by the teacher, by referring the learners to useful language lists or dictionaries, or by other learners. The task-based, procedural, negotiated, content-based, and skill-based syllabus are considered as process-oriented syllabuses.

Task-based syllabus: it is based on a list of the target language tasks that the learners need to learn to cope with the real-life situations such as passing a job interview and finding the address. **Procedural syllabus:** it contains learning tasks to be done rather than the language itself such as story-telling or map reading. It is claimed that structure can be best learned when attention is concentrated on *meaning*. The focus shifts from the linguistic aspect to the pedagogical one focusing on learning or the learner. The tasks and activities are designed and planned in advance but not the linguistic content.

Negotiated syllabus: it is a social and problem-solving model in which learners play the main role in determining how the language is learned and negotiation is the key concept.

Content-based syllabus: it is an approach in which teaching is organized based on the content rather than a linguistic syllabus. This content may come from science, literature, or history generated from an analysis of learners' interests and needs.

Skill-based syllabus: it is based on the content of the language teaching as a collection of specific abilities such as competences (pronunciation, vocabulary, grammar, and discourse) and skills (listening, writing, reading, and speaking) to develop language skills and competence.

Other possible syllabuses

Built-in syllabus: it focuses on the fact that learners should be exposed to those grammar features that they are ready to learn through a series of transitional stages.

Topic-based syllabus: it is completely topic-based including topics like "education"; it needs clear set of related vocabulary.

Notional syllabus: specific abstract notions like "time", "place", and "frequency" are used to express language.

Mixed or multi-strand syllabus: it contains topics, tasks, functions, notions, grammar, and vocabulary to make maximally helpful syllabus.

Cultural syllabus: it is based on considering culture and language as two inseparable and integral part of language learning.

It is important to bear in mind that all above mentioned syllabuses fit a specific context and purpose, and cater for specific learners with particular needs. It is wise to make an eclectic approach considering advantages of each approach and doing away with disadvantages of each one and trusting also in the evidence of your experience as a teacher.

Needs analysis in ELT

Needs Analysis (NA) is an important process before designing and evaluating lessons, materials, and syllabuses. It helps draw an outline to determine the needs for which students tend to learn English. Needs Analysis project points towards establishing the students' personal profile, motivational profile, needs and wants, lacks, target needs, learning styles and strategies, and strengths/weaknesses. In other words, needs analysis is the first step performed before a course and it is the process of establishing the "*what*" and the "*how*" of the course/syllabus. Nowadays needs analysis is an umbrella term that covers several approaches as follows:

1. **Target-situation analysis** is the model which aims at the learner's needs at the end of the course and target level performance.

2. **Present-situation analysis (PSA)** was proposed by Richterich and Chancerel (1997) and focuses on the learners' competence based on skills and language at the beginning of the course.

3. **Learning-centered approach** is a process of negotiation between learners and society, including syllabus, materials, teaching method etc., and may divide needs into necessities, lacks and wants.

4. **Strategy analysis** focuses on methods of learning i.e. preferred learning styles and strategies. Learning style is identified as any individual's preferred way of learning i.e. auditory, visual, kinesthetic/tactile, while learning strategy is the mental process the learner employs to learn the language.

5. **Deficiency analysis** shows existing proficiency against target learner proficiency representing deficiencies/lacks with the use of a three-point rating scale (none/some/lots), which determines the consideration that should be given.

6. **Means analysis** tends to study the local situation i.e. the facilities, teachers and teaching methods to see how the language course can be performed.

2. Lesson plan

The process of planning is a crucial dimension of teaching because the teacher creates ideas for a lesson based on learners' needs problems, interests, and understanding. Lesson planning is not necessarily in a written form but it can be considered as mental plans to organize the skeleton of teaching system.

Lesson plan is a description or outline of
1. **the goals** or **objectives** which have been set for a lesson.
2. **the activities and procedures** which will be used to achieve the goals.
3. **the time** which has been allocated to each activity.
4. **the order of activities** which will be followed.
5. **the materials** and **resources** which will be used during the lesson.

At the planning stage, the teacher faces a lot of questions, such as
- What will be the goals of the lesson?
- What materials will be used?
- What activities will be encouraged?
- What type of interaction will be maintained?

- How much time will be allocated to each activity?

Advantages of having a lesson plan

Advantages for students: evidence of a plan shows students that the teacher has devoted time to thinking about the class. It strongly suggests a level of professionalism and preparation. Lack of a plan may suggest the opposite of these teachers' attributes.

Advantages for the teacher: a plan gives the lesson a framework and an overall shape. It is true that the teacher may depart from the lesson plan at stages of the lesson, but he/she needs to have thought ahead, have a destination, and know how to get it.

An effective lesson plan has five stages

1. **Perspective (opening):** review of previous activities and preview of new lesson
2. **Stimulation:** preparing students for new activity
3. **Instruction:** presenting new activity
4. **Closure:** checking the students' learning
5. **Follow-up:** presenting opportunities for interaction

When implementing the lesson plan, teachers try to monitor the following issues

- Variety in teaching and choice of activity will keep the class interested and motivated.
- The varied activities should be coherent and well-organized.
- The harder activities and tasks should be placed earlier.
- Activities should not be too long or too short.
- There should be clear transition between activities.

There are some criteria to evaluate lesson effectiveness.

- The class seemed to learn the materials well.
- The learners were engaged in activities.
- The learners were attentive all the time.
- The lesson was interesting and enjoyable.
- The learners were active all the time.
- The lesson was designed according to a plan.

- The language was used communicatively.

There are several questions the teacher needs to consider while making an activity in a lesson plan.

1. **Who are the students for this activity?** It considers their age, level, cultural background, and individual characteristics.
2. **Why do you want to do it?** It considers purposeful and meaningful reasons for taking an activity.
3. **What will it achieve?** It considers aims provided behind the activity (to increase vocabulary for instance or fluency).
4. **How long will it take?** It considers needed time for activities.
5. **What will be needed?** It considers the equipment and materials required for activities.
6. **How does it work?** It considers the management of activities.
7. **How will it fit with what comes before and after it?** It considers the relevance of previous and subsequent tasks to new activities.

The lesson plan format

There is no fixed format for a lesson plan. The most important thing is that it should be useful for the teacher and for anyone who is observing him/her. Some teachers, for example, might write their plans on cards. Others will prefer handwritten sheets from a notepad; others will type them out immaculately on a word processor or do the planning inside their heads.

The pros and cons of unified teaching procedure
Advantages of implementing a unified procedure
- To make the concept of teaching more tangible
- To increase teachers' professionalism
- To systematize teaching
- To eliminate extreme variations from class to class
- To decrease confusion among students
- To consider students' different backgrounds, interests, learning styles, and abilities in one class
- To measure students' gains relatively easily

Disadvantages of not having a single procedure for all teachers:
- Teachers are not sure what is expected from them.

- Some teaching strategies may be left out.
- Students may become confused.
- Students may heavily prefer some teachers to others.
- Inexperienced teachers have no idea what to do and what is expected from them.
- If it is not managed well, criticism and negative evaluation may occur.

Sample English lesson plans

Teaching present simple tense
Objectives: by the end of this lesson, students will be able to

- ask and answer questions using present simple tense
- discuss present simple with "do and does"
- talk over everyday activities in communities/parks/reserves

Time: 25 minutes

Presentation 1: the **teacher** tells a story about what she does every day. Then he/she asks the students some questions about their routines. The teacher uses a calendar to show that events take place every day.

Teacher then presents the basic sentence structure:

I **eat** breakfast every day.	We **eat** breakfast every day.
You **eat** breakfast every day.	You **eat** breakfast every day.
It **eats** food every day.	They **eat** breakfast every day.
She **eats** breakfast every day.	He **eats** breakfast every day.

Practice: together the class and the teacher create some sentences about the everyday and habitual activities in [family] by brainstorming, "what does your father do every day?"

Presentation 1: if students are getting this quickly, you can now introduce the negative and question forms.

I **don't eat** eggs in the morning.

He **doesn't eat** rice in the morning.

Do you **eat** rice in the morning? **No, I don't.**

Does your sister **eat** cheese in the morning? **Yes, she does.**

Production 1: each student answers the question, "What do you do every day?" They each write some sentences. Then they present their responses to the class and discuss. They are encouraged to think about this in terms of conservation.

Presentation 2: the teacher asks questions with do, does and solicits responses. Then the teacher has students repeat the questions, now they know how to provide the responses.

Production 2: some students interview other students using questions similar to the followings:
"What do you do in the morning?"
"What do you do at night?"

3. Classroom Management

Another aspect of pedagogical dimension of teaching is the management of learners during the lesson. It contains increasing students' attention, maintaining their engagement in the lesson, and encouraging their motivation. If these aspects of a lesson are not well organized by a teacher, the teacher is not able to fulfill the goals of productive teaching.

Managing the teacher's role

The teacher has to manage a number of predictable situations as well as unpredictable ones. He/she has different roles at different times. For example:
- Asking or answering questions
- Designing of activities or material
- Eliciting language or language information
- Encouraging students
- Supporting students or up-front roles

The importance of classroom management
- It makes effective discipline.
- It considers preparation for the class.
- It encourages students' motivation.
- It provides a safe and comfortable learning environment.
- It increases students' self-esteem.
- It develops creativity in lesson delivery.
- It's different from one to one because of different teaching styles, personalities, and attitudes.
- It's influenced by the number of students.
- It increases students' desire for learning.
- It improves teachers' passion for teaching.
- It deals with handling time, space, material, auxiliary personnel and students.
- It changes the teacher's responsibility from controlling to managing.

Classroom management appreciates how to handle classroom learning and teaching to achieve productive ends. It deals with:

1. **Students' motivation**

2. **Constraints in the class**
3. **Teachers' role**

Factors influencing students' motivation

There are many issues that influence on students' motivation:

- National and cultural influences
- The state education system
- The classroom environment
- The school policy
- The text book
- The teacher
- The classmates

Motivating students

A. Creating the basic motivational conditions

a) Proper teachers' behavior and good teacher-student rapport
b) A pleasant and supportive classroom atmosphere
c) A cohesive learner group characterized by appropriate group norms

B. Generating student motivation

a) Increasing the learners' "goal-orientedness"
b) Making the curriculum relevant for the learners
c) Maintaining and protecting motivation
d) Encouraging language use through intensive and extensive motivation

The following ideas have worked in small and large classes to boost motivation.

- Using role-play
- Making pen friends
- Giving group presentations
- Making interclass debates
- Making speech competition
- listening to songs

Managing the constraints

The teacher should to be creative and patient to cope with constraints while teaching. The common classroom constraints follow as:

- Time limitation to finish the lesson
- Crowded classrooms to ask oral tasks and check written tasks individually
- Multilevel students to assign the same task
- Fixed furniture and decoration to control students while doing class activities
- Lack of photocopiers, DVD players, and video recorders to facilitate teaching and learning

Enhancing classroom climate in practice
Changing attitudes towards teachers and students

Teachers should believe that their major roles are to think, guide, initiate, facilitate and encourage the learners while learners are asked to increase their creativity and critical thinking skills.

Classroom set up

The classroom must be set up in a way to be organized, stimulating, and comfortable to create enthusiasm with colorful pictures, well-lit areas, movable chairs to do group activities, and established listening stations to use headsets in the case of silence necessity.

Over plan: if time is limited and you have too much to cover, avoid turning out of lessons and taking breaks.

Be consistent: moodiness is not suggested since it causes losing your students' attention and respect towards you.

Make rules understandable: students should understand what is and what is not acceptable. Further, the students should be aware of the consequences of breaking your rules beforehand.

Don't talk too much: use the first 15 minutes of class for lectures or presentations, and then get students to work.

Better classroom discipline: before starting your lesson, demand students' **attention**. While teaching, **monitor** their progress and provide examples of your own behavior as a **model** through **positive discipline**.

Talking and listening to students: showing an interest in what students have to say and encouraging discussion contributes to the students' language development.

Reasons for structuring group work

Structuring group work builds a sense of friendship and teamwork between students, promotes positive interdependence, involves students in learning, and provides more opportunities for personal feedback.

Techniques for better classroom control

- Be a kind mentor not a friend to earn students' trust by being firm, fair, and consistent.
- Be familiar with school policies before the course starts.
- Fill the period with learning activities by over planning.
- Give non-verbal clues to students.
- Learn students' names as soon as possible.
- Make silent learning occasionally.
- Make your instruction as clear as possible.
- Monitor students' progress.
- Move around the class to observe students' engagement in activities directly.
- Pay attention to all students.
- Show confidence in your teaching by being prepared.
- Show your students that you care about them.
- Speak with softer voice so that students really have to listen to what you're saying.

Classroom time budgeting

Allocated time to each activity or part should be based on the needs of the class and the importance of that activity. Time allocation should be logical.

Time management

Here are some strategies and tips on how to organize time management and classroom procedures before students work on the main learning task.

Assign homework to increase practice time. Doing homework allows students to practice skills they have already learned more at home because time is limited in the class.

Think of some aspects of school time you can control. In some schools, teachers discover that they can change the scheduling of class periods, pull-out programs, extracurricular activities planning time, and outside interruptions.

Schedule solid blocks of teaching time for each day. You might hang a "Do Not Disturb" sign outside your door to reduce disruptions.

Plan for smooth transitions between lessons and prepare materials for each lesson or activity. The teacher should make a plan for each activity in advance to make a coherent transition between lessons and stop wasting time.

Consider appropriate and flexible schedule breaks for maximum efficiency. A tactful teacher knows how to handle time deficiency with avoiding breaks.

Motivate students to improve classroom attendance. Attendance has a big effect on teaching and learning. Impress upon parents the importance of good attendance and teach an actual lesson on how it hurts to miss school.

Make yourself aware of the time in the class. As a teacher, wearing a watch can be helpful to make good time management.

Manage the discussion in the class. Give students allotted time to make discussion.

Don't make negative statement about time. Increase your time management abilities in your deeds. Stop nagging. Do not say there is lack of time.

Transition vs. allocated time

In order to manage your time in the class both allocated and transition time should be considered.

Allocated time: the time periods you *intend* to make students engaged in learning activities

Transition time: time periods that exist *between* allocated times for learning activities

Examples

- Getting students attention away from one activity to another
- Assigning an activity and directing it

Involvement in activities depends on how smoothly teachers move from one activity to another by increasing variety and decreasing transition time.

Withitness

It is the capacity of the teacher to be aware of what is going on in the classroom with accuracy and care. In the case of discipline problem, the teacher should be able to suppress the misbehavior decisively without disrupting the learning activity. When handling unexpected events verbally or non-verbally, the teacher should assure all students to learn what unacceptable behavior is.

Proximity and body language

In order to make an effective communication with students, the teacher should focus attention on eye contact, facial expressions, gestures, and physical proximity to students. Being free to roam and avoiding turning back to class must be taken seriously to show you are in calm control of the class.

Cooperation through communication

- *Never use sarcasm.*
- Verbalize feelings but remain in control.
- Do not place labels (good or bad).
- Do not get students hooked on praise.
- Praise the work and behavior – not the students themselves.
- Speak only to students when they are ready to listen.
- Prevent the activities of the class from disturbing other classes.
- Maintain acceptable standards of decorum among students, school personnel, and visitors to the school campus.

Seating arrangement

Make sure all students can see and hear clearly (and you can see them clearly). Teachers can set the chairs in different ways. Setting the chairs depends on size of the classroom, number of the students, and the purpose of activities done in the class. Here are some possibilities

- **Orderly rows:** the most classic format of classroom arrangement with a row between each desk and each desk facing the board
- **Circles:** arranging the desks evenly in a circle
- **Horseshoe:** placing the desks in a "U" Shape with students on the outside of the horseshoe facing inward
- **Separate tables:** three to five students around a table and in a group and the teacher controlling each group one by one

In circles, horseshoes, and especially, separate tables make a class less regimented and teacher-dominated, whilst recognizing that rows have their uses, and that the other arrangements are not without disadvantages.

- **Solowork:** each student working separately and the teacher passing among them while controlling the class

Arrangement should be done based on learning activities (lecture, class discussion, small group work, and pair work). In circles, horseshoes, and separate tables the class has less teacher domination, whilst row ordering is the most classical format and the teacher's role is distinct. In the figure 2.1 there are some practical classroom seating management.

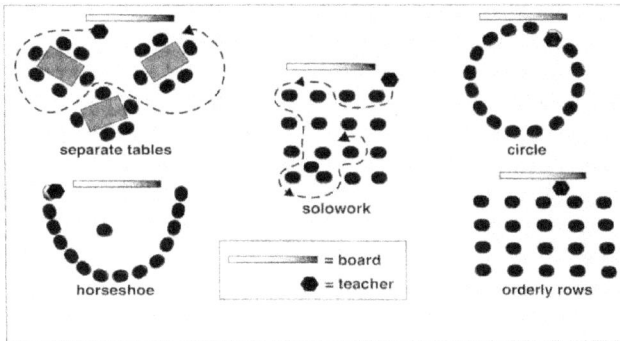

Figure 2.1 *Seating Management (Taken from Harmer, 2007)*

How to deal with misbehaviors
Finding causes of classroom misbehavior

Every behavior has a function. Much misbehavior is made because of teachers' or students' inappropriate behaviors. Do not tolerate undesirable behaviors no matter what the excuse. Understanding the function of a behavior will lead to knowing how to cope with that behavior. *Increase good behavior using rewards and positive reinforcement.* The followings are some primary reasons for disruptive behavior in the classroom:

1. **Getting attention:** the response to attention-seeking behavior should be fulfilled only if the student behaves properly.
2. **Struggling power:** the response to power seeking behavior is acknowledging the student's need.

3. **Seeking revenge:** revenge seeking students are angry and aggressive to hurt the teacher. The teacher should respond unexpectedly to surprise the rebellious student to reduce misbehaving.

4. **Avoiding inadequacy:** students will misbehave when they would rather appear 'bad' than appear inadequate in some way. The response to this behavior is within the context of a classroom climate where effort and growth can be valued more than the final product.

Verbal praise by teachers

In order to be an effective teacher, he/she should be consistent with personal, genuine, specific, and descriptive praise. The teacher can send home a note informing parents of their students' progress in lessons.

Punishment

Corporal punishment is not suggested at all since it causes anxiety and tension. Simply *a threat of resorting to certain punishment* or *verbal rebuke* can be effective.

Behaviors and possible responses
"Prevention is the best cure"

How to deal with ambling-wandering around and off the subject

Teachers can focus on relevant subjects and ask direct questions from rambling students. Using visual aids can be recommended. Teachers can ask directly from students to summarize their main points.

How to deal with side distraction conversations

It is not good to embarrass students. Teachers can casually move toward them or make eye contact to show you are willing to listen to them if they want to share their ideas on topic being discussed. As the last resort, you can stop and wait.

How to deal with shyness or silence- lack of participation

Teachers can change teaching strategies from discussion to writing by giving strong positive reinforcement for any distribution.

How to deal with sharpshooting

Teachers can ignore it or admit they don't know the answer and redirect the question to other students.

How to deal with arguing students-disagreeing with everything, making personal attacks

Teachers can redirect the question to group by recognizing students' feelings. It is good to acknowledge positive points while expressing your disagreement.

How to deal with grandstanding behaviors

Teachers should show their respects towards their ideas in a way that they are entitled to their opinion but time is limited to listen more to it.

How to deal with overt hostility/resistance

Teachers should remain calm by maintaining eye contact. It is not good to disagree but they can build on or around what has been said.

How to deal with complaining students

Teachers should point out that they can't change the policy but they can talk about the problem privately because of time pressure.

How to deal with a possible fight

Teachers can call for help. They can use the phone or ask administrators to handle it. It is good to document the incident in writing while everything is still fresh.

How to deal with someone disturbing the class

Teachers should resist giving attention to the disruptor. Proximity is a key of stopping such behavior. If it doesn't work, name the student while you are explaining the lesson to take attention. It is a good point that teachers determine what extreme misbehavior is.

How to deal with disruptions

In case of disruption, it is better to stop it with a little humor and avoid confrontations in front of others.

Dealing with other recurring problems
How to deal with apathetic behaviors

Some students just sit and do nothing productive. They look out the window, daydream, and do not do what they are supposed to do. It is necessary for teachers to be patient and organized to control the time and place by standing in front of students to increase motivation.

How to deal with off-task

It can be helpful to adapt lesson plans based on students' interests and talents to make more participation.

How to deal with students who do not use the target language

1- Motivate students to use the language properly

2- Ask them to answer only in English

3- Make an English environment

4- Localize topics

How to deal with students who come to class unprepared

1. Talk to your students about the importance of preparation.
2. Make assigned activities fun and use varied tasks.
3. Respect homework, check homework, and do important exercises in the classroom.

How to deal with students who do not talk in class

1- Use pair work (and group work) to provoke quiet students into talking.

2- Let them speak in a controlled way at first. Asking quiet students for instant fluency may be doomed to failure, initially.

3- Use role play since it is helpful. Many quiet students speak more freely when they don't have to be themselves.

Managing mixed-ability groups
Activities and strategies when students are all at different levels

Warm-up in whole group: starting your class with a whole-group warm-up is a great way to foster a sense of community in your multi-level class.

Information gap exercises: they work great for cross-ability and like-ability pairs.

Crossword puzzles: they work well for cross-ability pairs or small groups. Despite their low English vocabulary levels, each student will bring a wide variety of knowledge to the group to help fill in the puzzle.

Materials for self-Access: make sure everything is well labeled and organized. The materials should reflect the needs and interests of the students in your class.

Folktales: it is easy to find different levels of common folk or fairytales. They work well in children's classes, and there are even some that are appropriate for adults. The follow up activities for folktales are unlimited, but include comprehension questions, group discussions, vocabulary activities, creative writing exercise, and role-playing, all of which can be done in various groupings.

Art and images: visual stimuli can be great teaching tools. Use paintings as the basis for class discussions, writing assignments, and vocabulary building. Students of all different levels can participate together by describing photographs. Encourage students to bring in their own pictures and art and find ways to build lessons around them.

Assignments in computer lab: if your school has a computer lab for students to use, or if you have a computer in your classroom, allow pairs to do online English lessons.

Searching the best doer in group: if it is possible, use a wide variety of groupings to keep things interesting for your class.

Use of a simple schedule each day: make a routine in your activities such starting your class with warm-up and using pair work.

Isolating interested students to do peer tutoring: remind your students that the best way to practice and improve a new language is to teach it to someone else.

Use of different materials: when teachers know who the good and less good students are, they can form different groups to do different activities with different materials.

Different tasks with the same material: whenever teachers use the same material with the whole class, they can encourage students to do different tasks depending on their abilities.

Ignorance of problem: it is perfectly feasible to hold the belief that, within a heterogeneous group, students will find their own level. However, the danger of this position is that students will either be bored by the slowness of their colleagues or frustrated by their inability to keep up. The teacher should be creative in this case to stop boredom among students.

Use of students as assistants: some teachers adopt a strategy of peer help and teaching so that better students can help weaker ones. They can work with them in pairs or groups, explaining things, or providing good models of language performance in speaking and writing.

Managing large classes
Coping with large classes
Teachers' notebook: attach a small notebook and pen to your belt loop.

Take notes while you are monitoring pair or group learning. Review common errors as a whole group when an activity is completed.

Out-door activities: find another space that your class can use for energetic whole group activities. Take students outside if there is no indoor space available.

Creating a participation grade: make homework and attendance count by doing regular checks and making it part of their final grade. Giving a daily exam tip also encourages attendance.

Encouraging competition: establish a fun and competitive atmosphere within the class by dividing the class into teams.

Establishing trust: learn unique ways to remember names and do your best to know something about each of your students.

Managing the noise: establish a signal. Use it when you want your class to stop what they are doing and listen to you. Be careful not to use gestures or sounds that would offend anyone.

Decreasing marking and preparation time: design quizzes and tests in a way so that you can reduce the amount of marking. Use peer evaluations when possible.

Enforcing a policy: notify students of your policy on the first day and stick to it.

Sharing your e-mail address: encourage students to e-mail you with questions. Then answer them on your own time.

Using handouts and worksheets: one solution for teachers is to hand out worksheets for many of the tasks which they would normally do with the whole class if the class was smaller.

Using pair work and group work: in large classes, pair work and group work play an important part since they maximize student participation.

Using group reaction (conversation): since it becomes difficult to use a lot of individual repetition and controlled practice in a big group, it may be more appropriate to use students in chorus.

Using group leaders: teachers can enlist the help of a few group leaders. They can be used to hand out copies, check that everyone in their group (or row or half) has understood a task, collect work, and give feedback.

Activities in large classes

Discussions in small group: use topics related to a theme, or ask students to submit topic suggestions.

Finding out who you are: tape the name of a famous person to the back of each student. Students go around the room asking questions and trying to identify themselves.

Contests in team spelling: each student who gets the correct spelling receives a point for their team.

Balderdash: large class can be split into teams. The teacher calls out a word and students have to write down the part of speech and definition. Each student who gets both correct gets a point for his/her team.

Question writing: large class can be split into teams. The teacher calls out an answer and the students have to write the question.

Using questionnaires: students circulate around the room asking each other questions. Students can create their own questions on a given topic or theme, or the teacher can provide the questionnaire handout.

Categories: the teacher calls out a category, such as fruit, and each student has to name a fruit when it is his/her turn. If a student hesitates for more than five seconds, he/she has to choose a new category and sit out the rest of the game.

—

— Managing small classes

Coping with small classes

Using fillers: always have plenty of fillers (such as puzzles and games) ready in case activities finish quickly.

Reviewing: take the time to make sure that your students understand the lessons and material.

Encouraging confidence: help shy students feel more comfortable by trying not to put them on the spot.

Changing the dynamics: invite students from other classes once in a while. Prearrange pair group to know your activities with other teachers who have small classes.

Asking for feedback: take time to find out whether or not students are happy with the class. Put a question box or envelope out so that students can remain anonymous if they want to.

Small class activities

English newspapers: ask students to bring in a daily paper. Assign a part to each student to read and present.

Music in the classroom: have students listen to English songs. Use cloze exercises and teach vocabulary and idioms.

Story: have students tell stories from their own cultures or childhoods. It is fun to take students to a new location to do this, such as a park or a coffee shop.

Chain writing: each student writes one sentence on a piece of paper and then passes it on until each story is complete.

Role-playing: give students lots of opportunities to use the language they are learning in mock-style everyday settings.

Games: small groups are great for playing board games such as Word Up. Card games are a great way for students to practice asking questions. Make sure that they speak in English rather than speaking with gestures or in their own native language.

Online lessons: small classes can make use of computer labs easily. If your class does not have a computer lab, take students to the local library regularly to introduce them to the online learning sites.

Films: there are numerous lessons online for incorporating film into your class lessons. This can be done at all levels with great success, especially in a small class. Stop the film often in order to check comprehension and keep students focused.

Class excursions: take advantage of the class size, by getting out of the school as often as possible. Exposing students to real English outside of the classroom is one of the most important things you can do if they are visiting tourist attractions where there is the possibility of visiting English speakers.

Guest speakers: invite people into your classroom to speak or participate in a lesson. Your students will appreciate a new face from time to time in a class that has limited numbers.

Current research findings

Curriculum or course design is mostly a "how-to-do-it" practice that requires the integration of knowledge from different areas in the field of Applied Linguistics concerning language acquisition, teaching methodology, evaluation, language description, and materials production. Combining research and practice is applicable for ESL/EFL language education courses around the world.

Conclusion

In this chapter some ideas of the scope of syllabus design have been provided. Different possible syllabuses have been mentioned to make the possibility of taking eclectic approach through considering pros and cons of all syllabuses. In taking a particular approach needs analysis should not be ignored since it is an important factor that affects all aspects of teaching and learning course.

Teachers need to plan what they tend to do in their classrooms. There are different styles of teaching and planning. Lesson planning should not be considered as prescriptive planning. Teachers should have flexibility to plan in their own way. A clear lesson plan should maximize time and minimize confusion of students. Teachers should be receptive and flexible in the case of unforeseen problems. There are many ways of providing lesson plans. The main factor is to consider who the learners are. The pros and cons of unified teaching procedure have been discussed. Teachers should be aware of five stages of lesson planning to improve learning.

Classroom management is a crucial part of the classroom. Without classroom management, the teacher has no control over their classroom; which results in the students not learning well. Effective teachers can engage students, motivate them to do better, and create a comfortable environment conducive to learning all while effectively teaching students.

Teachers' physical presence and behavior in the classroom have been discussed. Teachers should know how to move and how to be close to the learners. Usefulness of gestures, facial expression should be considered. How to control different learners and how to arrange seating should not be ignored. Knowing how to punish learners is an important factor in teaching.

CHAPTER FIVE

Principles and Practices of Classroom Assessment
"Anything that exists in amount can be measured."   McCall

Introduction

Assessment in general, and language assessment in particular, is a challenging process. For one thing, assessments are used to make decisions which influence students' lives. Therefore, assessment must provide as accurate information as possible to enable teachers to make fair decisions. For another thing, assessment is a very complex responsibility. Assessment is a major consideration in any educational settings. Teachers have always wanted to know how much their students have learned. Students, administrators, and parents all work toward achieving educational goals. Measurement and assessment are crucial tools to help them reach most of these objectives to make sound educational decisions.

Differences between Measurement, test, and evaluation

Measurement is the process which includes assigning numbers to both physical and mental characteristics of people based on explicit rules and procedures. It means that in measurement three factors of **quantification** (assigning some numbers), **characteristics** (directly or indirectly observed), and **rules and procedures** (avoiding blind or haphazard assignment of numbers to the characteristics) should be considered. Rankings, rating scales, and tests are some types of measures in the social sciences.

Test is a measurement tool to elicit an individual's specific sample of behavior. Language tests should be reliable, meaningful, and useful.

 Evaluation is defined as the systematic gathering of information to make decisions. It can be qualitative or quantitative and it does not necessarily cover testing.

Assessment and testing

Assessment is an ongoing process that contains a wide range of techniques. All the students' activities in the class and all the teachers' appraisal of the students' performance can be considered as assessment. **Testing**, on the other hand, is a subset of assessment.

Main purposes of assessment

- To provide teachers with feedback on students' progress
- To provide students with educative feedback
- To give motivation to students
- To make a record of students' progress
- To create a form of certification
- To evaluate students' readiness for future learning

Types of assessment

Formative assessment: it promotes effective learning by students (assessment for learning). It evaluates students in the process of learning competences and skills in order to help them to continue the growth of the process. All kinds of informal assessment are formative.

Summative assessment: it identifies what a student has learned at the end of a course or unit of instruction (assessment of learning). Final exams are examples of summative assessment.

Norm-referenced assessment: it shows each student's performance in relation to the performance of others. It does not directly tell us what the student is capable of doing in the language.

Criterion-referenced assessment: it refers to grading of each student's performance in terms of whether a particular description of performance has been met. The purpose is to clarify students based on whether or not they are able to perform tasks satisfactorily. The tasks are set, and those students who perform well *"pass"*; those who do not *"fail"*.

Internal assessment: the assessment activities are made by the class teachers. Internal assessment is an integral part of the course. It enables students to represent the application of their skills and knowledge, and to follow their personal interests, without the time limitations and other constraints that are related to written examinations. The internal assessment should be woven into normal classroom teaching and not be a separate activity set after a course has been taught.

External assessment: external assessments are made, chosen, and controlled by another person or group such as commercial publishers, national administrators, or policymakers. Typical examples of external assessments contain standardized and commercial reading tests. External assessments are administered less frequently than internal assessments, but they usually have greater importance.

Authentic assessment

Simply assessing an isolated skill or a retained fact does *not* effectively measure a student's capabilities. To accurately evaluate what a student has learned, an assessment method must examine his/ her *collective abilities*. The term **authentic assessment** describes the multiple forms of assessment that can reflect students' learning, achievement, motivation, and attitudes on instructionally relevant classroom activities. *Authentic assessment links between the real language use and test tasks.* All content and skills under test should mirror as exactly as possible the factor of *authenticity*. E.g. in a reading comprehension test, the test maker should choose passages that match topics the test-taker may read outside of the testing situation.

Authentic assessment generally accomplishes the following goals:

- It focuses on what students know, rather than what they do not know.
- It makes students develop responses instead of selecting them from predetermined options.
- It directly evaluates holistic projects.
- It applies samples of student work collected over an extended period of time.
- It uses clear criteria made known to students and parents.
- It makes higher-order thinking.
- It allows for the possibility of multiple human judgments.
- It relates more closely to classroom Learning.
- It emphasizes on the differences in learning styles, language proficiencies, cultural and educational backgrounds, and grade levels.

Functions of tests

Tests serve two main functions (the purpose for which a test is designed):

Prognostic tests: they are predictive tests that identify learning difficulties or problem. They show learners' strengths and weaknesses to ascertain what learning still needs to take place. They are not related to learners' educational background.

1. **Selection tests:** they provide information about examinees' acceptance or non-acceptance into a particular program. The criterion for pass or fail is made by the authorities. There should not be any limitation for examinees who obtain the score. If the number of applicants passing a test is more than the capacity of the educational programs the selection test becomes a competition test like the Entrance Examination for universities in Iran.

2. **Placement tests:** they are placing new students in the appropriate classes. Typically they are used to assign students to classes at different levels. There is no pass or fail in placement tests. The purpose of placement tests is to measure the capabilities of an examinee in following a particular path of language learning.

3. **Aptitude tests:** they contribute to making decisions on the future career of the examinees. They are designed to measure general ability to learn a foreign language before taking a course.

Evaluation of attainment tests: in contrast to prognostic tests, these tests are based on the extent to which examinees have learned the materials they have been taught.

1. **Achievement tests:** they measure students' language progress as *final achievement tests* administered at the end of the course or *progress achievement tests* during the course. They are either *general* to cover the knowledge that the test takers should achieve based on a particular course or *diagnostic* to determine the strengths or weaknesses of the test takers in a special course of study.

2. **Proficiency tests:** they are designed to measure people's language knowledge and ability regardless of any training courses that candidates may have previously taken.

3. **Knowledge tests:** they are designed to be used in situations where the medium of instruction is a language other than the examinees' mother tongue to measure knowledge in areas other than the language itself.

Discrete point versus integrative testing

Discrete-point testing: it evaluates each item of language separately at a time. *Gap fills* such as single sentence, cloze, multiple choices, using given words, sentence transformation, sentence construction, and reconstruction and *two-option answers* such as true or false, and correct or incorrect items are considered as discrete-item testing.

Integrative testing: it measures the actual aspects of activities in using language simultaneously. It combines many language elements to complete a task. It involves writing a composition or taking a dictation. Some common integrative tests are cloze, dictation, and composition writing.

Direct versus indirect testing

Direct testing: it refers to test formats which duplicate the setting and performing of the real life situations. Writing samples and oral interviews are referred to as direct tests.

Indirect testing: it is measuring the abilities that underlie the skills in which the teacher is interested. It does not require the test takers' language in use. An inference can be made from learners' performances on more artificial tasks.

Computer adaptive testing: it provides all candidates with an item of *average difficulty*. Those who can answer well are presented with a more difficult item; those who respond incorrectly are given an easier item.

Communicative language testing: it is believed that in order to make a special language test useful, test performance must correspond to language use in non-test situations. Communicative language teaching makes use of real-life situations that need communication. The teacher sets up a situation that learners encounter in real life. The real-life simulations should change from day to day. Learners' motivation to learn comes from their interest to communicate in meaningful ways about meaningful topics.

Test development stages

In order to make effective classroom-based tests the followings should be considered:

- The clear and unambiguous purpose and objective of the test should be made in advance.
- The characteristics of the setting such as physical characteristics, participants, location, noise level; lighting, materials, and needed time should be considered.
- The test-maker should make clear all the related rubrics such as the content, explicit instruction, number of tasks, sequence of tasks, importance of tasks, the item types (multiple-choice, essay- type

items, etc.), tasks that should be based on the target language use, needed skills, structural range, vocabulary range, dialect, accent, style, scoring method, feedback, and the way of reporting the result of the test to students.

- The test-maker should define the format of the tasks. It contains the channel (aural, visual), form (language, non-language, both), language (native, target, both), length, type, and degree of speededness.

Item form classification

The item formats are categorized in different groups:

- **Subjective items** such as translation that does not have any systematic scoring procedures.
- **Objective items** such as multiple-choice and true-false tests that follow objective criteria.
- **Essay-type items** that the students are required to produce language elements.
- **Suppletion items** can focus on supplying the missing parts.
- **Recognition items** are the opposite of suppletion. They include objective or multiple-choice items.
- **Multiple-choice items** have many forms, but the basic form has a stem and a number of options. One option is correct and the others are distractors.

The structure of an item

The smallest unit of a test is an item. It has two parts:

The stem elicits information from the test-taker. It can be prepared as a question, a statement, or other linguistic constructions.

Here are some examples.

1. What is the purpose of face validity?
2. A direct test refers to ....

The response is the information which is elicited from the test-taker. It can range from choosing a single word to producing an essay.

Two kinds of tests

Teacher-made tests: usually do not have uniform directions. The sampling and the content are determined by the teacher. The quality of the test may be poor because it is prepared haphazardly without item analysis or revision. It is suitable for intraclass comparisons.

Standardized tests: they are prepared based on particular instructions, high quality administration, and specific scoring procedures. The sampling and the content are done systematically by experts. Item analysis and item revisions are integral parts of designing the tests. They are used for interclass and national comparisons.

Key terms in standardized tests
Characteristics of an individual item

Item facility/difficulty

Item facility (IF) refers to easiness of an item. It is one of the most important characteristics of an item. To calculate item facility all correct responses should be divided by the total number of responses. An item facility should be between zero to one. Too easy or too difficult items are not recommended since they do not provide useful information about the test-takers' knowledge. Item facility below 0.37 is too difficult and more than 0.63 is too easy.

$$IF = \frac{\sum C}{N} = \frac{\text{sum of the correct responses}}{\text{total number of responses}}$$

Item discrimination

Item discrimination (ID) refers to the extent to which an item discriminates more knowledgeable examinees from less knowledgeable ones. It discriminates between weak and strong test-takers. There is a relationship between IF and ID. An item with too high or too low IF has less discrimination power. To calculate ID

- rank total scores from highest to lowest.
- divide test-takers into two equal groups.
- compute the ID through the following formula

$$ID = \frac{CH - CL}{1/2N}$$

CH: test-takers' number of correct answers to a particular item in the high group

CL: test-takers' number of correct answers to a particular item in the low group

N: total number of answers

Choice distribution

Choice distribution refers to the effectiveness of the frequency of the choices. If from 20 items in a multiple-choice test, as an example, 18 test-takers choose the correct answer which is item B, nobody chooses item A, nobody chooses item C, and 2 test-takers choose item D, the distractors should be modified because they are distributed poorly.

Characteristics of items altogether

Test-makers can test anything that they have taught; it means the four language skills and the components. It should have all factors of reliability, validity, authenticity, practicality, washback, and interactiveness. A good test should be fair and appropriate for students. It shouldn't be too troublesome to score. It should make clear and purposeful results. A classroom test shouldn't be a time to introduce new tasks but a form that students have practiced and feel comfortable with. The followings are some characteristics of a good test based on considering all items together.

Practicality

A test should be usable and practical in terms of ease of interpretation, making, giving, and scoring. These contain costs, amount of time, human resources, and material resources needed to administrate a test.

Reliability

A reliable test yields similar results if it is given to the same students or matched students on two different occasions. It is the quality of test scores. It deals with true score that is due to an individual's level of ability not error score that is due to other factors. It is possible to measure the reliability of a test through **reliability coefficient** which makes it possible to compare the reliability of different tests. The test **reliability** coefficient can be found between 1 to 0.

There are some key terms in statistics, which involves collecting numerical information, analyzing information, and making meaningful decisions based on the results of the analyses. These definitions are used in testing and should be learned before estimating reliability as well. Your students may like to know how they performed on a test. The measures of the following terms will help gain useful information before measuring reliability.

1. **The mode** refers to the most frequent score in a set of score.
2. **The median** (MD) refers to the score that divides the set of scores into equal parts.
3. **The mean** ($\bar{x}$) refers to the average of the scores.
    $$\bar{x} = \frac{\Sigma x}{N} = \bar{x} = \frac{\text{sum of scores}}{\text{number of scores}}$$
4. **Range** refers to the difference between the largest number in a set of scores and the smallest one.
5. **Variance** refers to the extent the scores differ from the mean. It can be calculated through the use of the following formula:
    $$V = \frac{\Sigma(X - \bar{x})^2}{N - 1}$$
6. **Standard deviation** refers to the square of the variance.
    $$S = \frac{\sqrt{\Sigma(X - \bar{x})^2}}{N - 1}$$

Reliability estimation

Reliability can be considered as the consistency of scores made by a given test. The degree of the error measurement can cause unreliability. There are different methods to estimate reliability:

*   **Test-retest method** is giving a group of test-takers the same test twice. The gap between two administrations should not be too long or too soon. Therefore, around two weeks can be acceptable.
*   **Alternative forms (or parallel forms)** can be using two different forms of the same test to a group of test-takers just one time.
*   **Split half method** is splitting or dividing a homogeneous test into two equal halves given to a group of test-takers once.
*   **Rational-equivalence reliability (KR-21 method)** is the easiest and the most practical way to estimate reliability because there is no need for double administration and parallel forms of a test to split the test into two halves.
    $$(\text{KR-21}) \; r = \frac{K}{K-1} \cdot \frac{\bar{x}(K - \bar{x})}{KV}$$

K = the number of the items in a test
$\bar{x}$ = the mean score
V = the variance

Factors contributing to reliability

- **Reliability related to learners:** learners' anxiety, fatigue, and illness and other physical, psychological issues may cause error scores that are deviant from true scores.

- **Reliability related to raters:** lacking scoring criteria and inexperienced raters may cause subjectivity and bias to enter into the scoring process.

- **Reliability related to test administration:** poor conditions of desks, photocopying variations, and the amount of light cause unreliability.

- **Reliability related to test construction:** too long or too short tests cause unreliability. Subjective tests such as speaking assessment or writing composition have less reliability than a well-organized multiple-choice test. A test with 75 items can be acceptable to have satisfactory reliability.

Speed tests: the items in these tests are relatively easy and are based on the ability level of the test-takers. There is limited time that few test-takers can complete all items. The score represents only the speed with which the test-taker can work. It does not determine the test-taker's ability or knowledge. To calculate reliability for speed tests, test-retest and parallel tests can be used.

Power tests: in these tests item difficulty increases gradually but with enough time to allow everyone to answer all the questions. Power tests include too difficult items so no one can get a perfect score. To calculate reliability for power tests, split half method can be used.

Validity

A valid test measures exactly what it proposes to measure without irrelevant variables. It offers useful, meaningful information about test-takers' ability. It must be supported by a theoretical rationale. There are different kinds of validity:

- **Content validity:** a test has content validity if its content makes a representative sample of the language skills, structures, etc.

- **Criterion-related validity:** it relates to the extent to which test results agree with those received by some independent and extremely dependable assessment of the learner' ability.

- **Construct validity:** it refers to the underlying ability which is hypothesized in a theory of language ability.
- **Face validity:** a test has face validity if it shows what it is supposed to measure.
- **Consequential validity:** it refers to the changes that may happen based on test scores interpretation.

Relationship between reliability and validity

If a test is valid, it must be reliable. If students receive very different scores on a test every time they take it, the test is not likely to predict anything. However, if a test is reliable, that does **not** mean that it is valid. Reliability is a necessary, but not sufficient, condition for validity.

Authenticity

Authenticity refers to natural language, contextualized items, meaningful, relevant, interesting topics, thematic organization, and relative real-world task. Teachers shouldn't ignore the importance of authenticity and naturalness in making context and items for a test.

Washback

Whashback refers to the impact of testing on teaching and learning. The effect can be positive, negative, summative, or informative.

Interactiveness

Interactiveness refers to involvement of test-takers' characteristics in completing a test. It includes test-takers' language ability, language knowledge, strategic competence (how well a learner uses verbal forms and non-verbal communication to make up for lack of knowledge) affective factors (emotion including curiosity, excitement, enthusiasm, flexibility, skepticism, and open-mindedness) and knowledge of the world.

Assessing language components and skills

1. Vocabulary assessment

Nature of vocabulary
- **Tokens** mean all words in a text.
- **Types** mean only words that are of different forms not that repeated ones.

- **Function words** belong to the grammar of the language than vocabulary.
- **Content words** are nouns, verbs, adjectives, and adverbs. They can be used for testing vocabulary.
- **Phrasal verbs** ("drop off"), **compound nouns** ("target like"), **idioms** ("wet blanket"), and **prefabricated language** are groups of words that have a grammatical structure but operate as a single unit. They are **poly words** (short fixed phrases functioning as quantifying, marking fluency, disagreement, etc. For example: wait a minute, **Institutional expressions** (longer utterances such as proverbs), **Phrasal constraints** (medium-length phrases with basic structure with one or two slots filled by different words or phrases. For example: yours truly/sincerely, and **Sentence builders** (phrases provide the framework with one or two slots to complete a sentence. For example: I am afraid of X.

Principles for constructing vocabulary items

- Clarify your purpose.
- Define your construct.
- Select the target words.
- Determine mode of performance. *Receptive* (recognition, matching exercise, and word association) or *productive* (recall and fill-in-the-blank).
- Make a clear context.
- Don't include any grammatical structure.
- Don't use difficult context.
- Choose easier choices than the word being tested.
- Select distractors and the word being tested of the same level of difficulty.
- Make choices with the same length.

2. Grammar assessment

Grammatical knowledge

There are three interrelated elements. **Grammatical forms** (morphology and syntax related to accuracy of language), **grammatical meanings** (literal and intended meaning), and **pragmatics meaning** (the appropriate language choices in a communicative event).

- **Selected response** including *multiple-choice tasks* (the most common selected response task includes a blank or underlined words in a sentence and the correct answer should be chosen), and *discrimination tasks* (such as true /false), *noticing tasks or consciousness-raising tasks* (underling or circling a specific feature in the language).
- **Limited production** including *gap-filling tasks* (in a form of a sentence, dialogue, or passage with a number of deleted words), *short-answer tasks* (presented in the form of a question), and *dialogue-completion tasks* (a short of conversation in which a part of the exchange is blank).
- **Extended production** including *information gap tasks* (input in terms of incomplete information), and *role-play or simulation* (test-takers are asked to take on a role to solve a problem).

Principles for testing structure

- Include a natural dialog for the stem of the item.
- Make sure that each item has only one acceptable answer.
- Make alternatives brief to the point.
- Provide sufficient context for the stem.
- Prepare options based on equal size.

3.   Listening assessment

Listening performance and related tasks

Listening can be tested as a skill on its own, although in real life it occurs with speaking. There are four identified types of listening performance which should be considered in listening assessment.

- **Intensive** refers to listening to perceive phonemes, words, intonation, and discourse markers. Tasks include recognizing phonological and morphological elements from two or more choices, and paraphrase recognition by providing a stimulus sentence and having the test-taker choose the true paraphrase from a number of choices.
- **Responsive** refers to listening to a short stretch of language to make a short response. Tasks are choosing an appropriate response to a question or open-ended response to a question.

- **Selective** refers to listening to look for general meaning to comprehend designated information in a longer context of spoken language. Tasks are listening cloze with listening to a story, monologue, or conversation in order to complete a written text containing some blanks, information transfer in which aural information must be transferred to visual pictures, such as labeling a diagram, and sentence repetition which means repeating a sentence as an assessment of listening comprehension.

- **Extensive** refers to listening to develop global understanding of lengthy lecture and conversation. Tasks are applying dictation, and communicative stimulus-response tasks which include a conversation with a set of comprehension questions.

What makes listening difficult?

There are a lot of reasons that make listening difficult. **Clustering** means attending to appropriate chunks of language, **redundancy** means recognizing repetitions, rephrasing, and elaborations, **reduced forms** mean understanding the reduced forms that are not in formal textbooks, **colloquial language** means comprehending idioms, slang, and reduced forms. Discourse markers mean understanding words such as "next", "secondly", **rate of delivery** means keeping up with the speed of delivery, **intonation, rhythm, and stress**, and **interaction** means interactive flow of listening to speaking to listening.

Authentic listening tasks

- **Notetaking** can be used in the academic world and classroom lectures. It is based on listening and writing skills.

- **Editing** needs both a written and a spoken stimulus. It means test-takers read the written material for example a news report, then they hear a spoken version of the stimulus that deviates from the original written form. Finally test-takers show the difference between the two versions.

- **Interpretive tasks** need all four language skills. They are based on paraphrasing a story or conversation.

- **Retelling** relates to listening to a story or news to retell or summarize it.

Principles for constructing pronunciation items

- Use informal spoken materials with very high frequency.
- Choose points in the English language that have no counterparts in students' native language.
- Don't test phonemes of the language in isolation.
- Record examinees' spoken answers in production tests.

Principles for testing listening comprehension

- Select pictures with great care.
- Use real-life spoken stimuli.
- Construct questions on dialogs with two possible objectives
  1. Ask about overall comprehension.
  2. Introduce a problem.
- Avoid using outside knowledge in the oral stimulus.
- Choose options free from any grammatical or lexical difficulty.
- Present oral stimuli either live or played with DVD player.

4. Speaking assessment

Types of speaking tasks

- **Imitative** types refer to the ability to imitate a word or phrase. Tasks are word and sentence repetition.

- **Intensive** types refer to the production of short and limited stretches of oral language through directed response tasks to elicit a particular grammatical form, read-aloud tasks include reading beyond the sentence level up to paragraphs. Teachers record the test-takers' output to score it based on scoring scales, sentence/dialog completion tasks and oral questionnaires which require test-takers to read dialogs with omitting one speaker's lines. The test-takers should fill in the omitted part; picture-cued tasks are used to elicit oral language performance, and translation.

- **Responsive** types refer to brief interactions with interlocutors through question and answer, giving instruction and directions, and paraphrasing.

- **Interactive types** refer to transactional language and interpersonal exchanges through interview, role play, discussion and conversations, and games.

- **Extensive (monologue) types** refer to speeches, oral production, and storytelling. Related tasks are oral presentations, picture-cued storytelling, and retelling a story (Brown & Abeywickrama, 2010).

Principles for testing oral production

- Make natural and realistic interviews.
- Utilize the services of at least two raters.
- Put the interviewee at ease.
- Make a specific scoring procedures based on accent, structure, vocabulary, fluency, and comprehension.
- Try to record the interview.

5. Reading assessment

Types of reading tasks

Here are some suggestions for reading comprehension assessment

- **Perceptive** reading tasks focus on the components of stretches of reading text such as letter, words, and punctuation, and bottom-up processing.
- **Selective** reading tasks focus on recognizing lexical, grammatical, or discourse features through picture-cued tasks, matching, and multiple-choice.
- **Interactive** reading tasks refer to bringing the reader to the text to understand it and negotiate the meaning through anecdotes, short narratives, descriptions, memos, and announcement.
- **Extensive** reading tasks refer to texts more than a page including articles, essays, short stories, and books to tap into a learner's global understanding of a text

Principles for constructing reading comprehension

- Use samples with language learning objectives.
- Choose suitable, culturally fair, and interesting subjects.
- Select passages of 100 to 300 words.
- Make open-ended or multiple-choice items.
- Illustrate clearly the lead of the item.
- Avoid choices with "all of the above", "none of the above", "both A and B", or "neither A nor B".

- Avoid items with clues to the right answer.
- Make items which need thorough understanding of the reading materials.

6. Writing assessment

Types of writing tasks

- **Imitative** tasks refer to producing written language based on letters, words, punctuation, and brief sentences. Copying, picture-cued tasks, completion tasks, converting numbers and abbreviations to words, spelling tasks, matching phonetic symbol are from imitative tasks.

- **Intensive** (controlled) tasks refer to producing appropriate vocabulary in a context with correct grammatical features based on focusing on form through dictation, grammatical transformation tasks, and picture description.

- **Responsive** tasks require learners to make paragraph writing through paraphrasing, topic sentence writing, topic development within a paragraph, development of main and supporting ideas across paragraphs, reports, summaries of readings/videos/lectures, narration, and description.

- **Extensive** tasks refer to using all the processes and strategies of writing an essay, a term paper, and a research project report (Brown & Abeywickrama, 2010).

Principles for making writing tests

- Avoid vague topics.
- Identify real life writing situations.
- Make worded items to show what is expected.
- Choose the same writing task for all examinees.
- Change one long composition to two shorter ones.
- Do not consider irrelevant skills of art in scoring.

Cloze test and dictation

Cloze test: it is any passage with appropriate length and difficulty with some word deleted. Standard cloze tests have every 7th word deleted with 25-30 numbers of deletions in a passage between 175-210 words.

Dictation: it is considered as integrated tests. Language is measured as a holistic manner. Recent research indicates that dictation is one of the highly valid and reliable language proficiency measurements. The modern use of dictation is different from its traditional treatment. Dictation in the past introduced the text word-by-word or chunk-by-chunk. Nowadays dictation has led to the development of standard dictation.

Standard dictation: it refers to a passage with appropriate length, difficulty, and administration procedure. The length of dictation should be about 100-150. The level of difficulty, like in cloze test is important to be considered. It is believed that the passage should be a little below the students' level of language proficiency. Dictation administration should follow special conventional procedures.

Principles for dictation

- Dictation is generally read and the students are asked to write down what they hear.
- The reader should have consistency in the manner of reading.
- Recording the passage in advance alleviates inconsistency in accents, pronunciation, pauses, articulation, and supersegmental variations.
- Dictation should be read three times.
- The first reading gives students a chance to get general ideas of the passage, while they are not allowed to write down anything.
- The second reading should be at a normal rate, because students have to write down the passage.
- The third time is somehow like the first time. Students check their writing.
- In all three readings, normal rate of speech should be considered.

Different forms of dictation

- **Partial dictation** is a passage with some deletions and students are asked to fill in the deleted parts as they listen to the passage.
- **Elicited dictation** is asking students to imitate what they hear. It is not in written form but in oral form.
- **Dicto-comp** is the combination of dictation and composition. The passage is given to students as a whole and students are required to compose the text they hear.

Test scoring

There are two types of scoring

1. **Objective scores:** they are scores a person receives on a multiple choice, true-false, or matching question in an exam.
2. **Subjective scores:** they refer to scores a person receives on short response questions, extended response question, or essays.

Marking subjective tests

There are a number of solutions to marking subjectively.

- Training the scorers to reduce biases, increase accuracy of evaluations, improve behavioral accuracy to increase observational skills, and finally boost scorers' confidence.
- Employing more than one scorer to decrease the level of unreliability based on poor judgment.
- Using global assessment scales to establish a rating procedure and determining the criteria for judging. It should contain various components of language competence and performance such as fluency, accuracy, , and appropriateness of sociocultural organization.

Assessment activities in the classroom

Assessment activities are integral part of teaching and learning a new language. The main classroom assessment activities are

- **Monitoring class work activities:** teachers should monitor all students' progress repeatedly and investigate students' understanding and difficulties.
- **Assigning homework:** homework tasks are very important in making feedback about how well a student can perform when unaided.
- **Using teacher-made tests:** short tests devised by teachers can motivate learning in preparation for the test.
- **Taking formal examinations:** these kind of internal assessment tests tend to develop examination skills and techniques.

Carrying out assessment activities

A number of important points are needed to be considered in carrying out assessment activities

- The assessment activities should be fair related to the materials covered.
- The assessment activities should be related to the school planning.

- The program of assessment activities used over a long period of time should be varied.
- Students should be informed about time, nature, and purpose of the assessment.
- The administrators should try to facilitate testing by avoiding disruptions and minimizing students' anxiety.
- The instructions should be clear without ambiguity.
- The assessment activities should assess validity.

Recording students' progress

Making a good record of students' progress has three main functions.

1. It provides a helpful basis from which reports to others can be made.
2. It highlights a mark drop compared with previous progress.
3. It facilitates the planning of future work with each student.

Reporting students' progress

Giving feedback to students about their progress is very important in creating motivation and further progress. Teachers' comments on reporting could be about students' ability, attitude, confidence, effort, behavior, examination results, homework, attendance, and participation.

Feedback

There are two types of feedback used by teachers. They can be positive, neutral, and negative. **Affective feedback** is based on teachers' feeling about students' language production while **cognitive feedback** is considered as teachers' understanding of students' message.

Teachers' problems in writing school reports

- It relies on subjective judgments.
- It is not easy to summarize students' performance in a meaningful form to the reader.
- Giving honest report makes tension for teachers.

Teachers' assistance in making effective classroom tests

Teachers should help students learn some strategies to decrease a sleepless night full of anxiety before taking a test. Here are some points:

Principles for test-makers

1. **Before taking the test:** teachers should give all necessary information about the test. They can make a review of material before the test and caution students to have a good night's rest. Students should not forget to attend the class early to reduce stress.

2. **During the test:** students need to have a quick look over the whole test as soon as the test is distributed. They should estimate the needed time to answer the test. While answering, they should be advised to concentrate as much as they can. Before the end of the test period, teachers should give students a few minutes to proofreading the answers.

3. **After taking the test:** when returning the test results, teachers should give feedback on the parts that students did not do well and advise students to make a plan to focus attention in the future to points that they are not good at.

What should be graded in the classroom?

There are some factors which can be graded in an English classroom

- Students' language performance on tests and quizzes
- Informal observation of students' performance
- Students' oral participation in class
- students' improvement over the course
- Students' behavior such as being polite, active, disruptive, etc.
- Students' effort and hardworking in learning English
- Students' motivation, attendance, and punctuality

Expressing grades in language components and skills

There are various possibilities to express the grades which teachers give the students at the end of the course

- Absolute grading: grading based on numerical point system grading
- Relative grading: grading based on ranking students (percentile ranks)
- Evaluative comment expression: "Well done"
- Profiles expression: comprising grades on different skills in detail
- letters, words or phrase: "A" (the top 25 percent of scores) , "B" (the next 25 percent),"C" (the next 25 percent), and "D" (the lowest 25 percent)

Principles for grading

- Grading is not a universally accepted scale.
- Generally, grading is subjective and depends on the context.
- Often grading is done on a curve.
- Grades show teachers' philosophy of testing.

Guidelines for grading

- Make an informal grading philosophy consistent with your teaching philosophy.
- Choose suitable criteria for grading.
- Communicate with students about the criteria used for grading at the beginning of the course.
- Give grades to students privately.
- Discuss grades individually with learners.

What is grading on a curve?

Some teachers use curves to grade exams, while others prefer to assign grades with the percentages. Most of the time, this type of grading boosts the students grade. The "curve" referred to the "bell-curve," used in statistics to show the distribution of any set of data. In a normal distribution, most of the data are near the mean.

How do teachers grade on a curve? There are a number of ways to grade on a curve:

- **Add points:** a teacher tops off each student's grade with the same number of points.
- **Bump a grade to 100%:** a teacher moves one kid's score to 100% and adds the same number of points used to get that kid to 100 to everyone else's score.
- **Use the square root:** a teacher takes the square root of the test percentage and makes it the new grade.

Grading writing

There is a set of criteria to grade intermediate to advanced students' writing objectively. In writing assessment organization, content, use of grammar, vocabulary, and punctuation and spelling should be considered as important factors.

	20-18 Excellent to good	17-15 Good to Adequate	14-12 Adequate to fair	11-6 Unacceptable	5-1 Not good
organization	Good title, introduction, body, and conclusion	Adequate title, introduction, body, and conclusion	Problem in ordering ideas	Severe problems in ordering of ideas	No effort to organize the composition
Content	Concrete ideas	Extraneous material	Incomplete paragraph development	Inadequate effort in area of content	No apparent effort to consider the topic
Grammar	Native-like grammar	Some grammar problems	Apparent Grammar problems	Serious grammar problems	Unintelligible structure
Vocabulary	Precise vocabulary	Good vocabulary	Lack of good vocabulary	Problem in vocabulary	Inappropriate use of vocabulary
Punctuation and spelling	Correct use of English writing conventions	Some problems with writing conventions	Using general writing conventions	Serious problems with format of writing	Disregarding English writing

Table 5. 1 *Analytic Scale for Rating (Adapted from Brown & Bailey, 1984, pp. 39-41)*

Grading Speaking

Many English teachers prefer to test grammar or lexis with pen and paper test. They think testing speaking is challenging. Here are some ideas.

- Prepare criteria.
- Extend your assessment over a few lessons, in case of a large class.
- Use speaking tasks (narrating a picture story, playing roles, etc.).

Common format in grading oral testing

The examiner can make criteria for speaking assessment through classifying the examinee's ability in expressing the topic during speaking assessment. The followings represent the variety of abilities. Based on the examinee's ability the rater can grade the speaking assessment.

1. The examinee does not speak at all.
2. The examinee uses single-word responses.
3. The examinee responds in brief phrases.
4. The examinee can use short sentences.
5. The examinee use longer sentences.
6. The examinee speaks fluently.

Alternative Assessment Procedures

It has been described as an alternative to standardized testing and all of the weaknesses found with such tests. It is different from traditional testing since it actually asks students to present what they can do. Reliability or consistency in alternative assessment is often ensured through *triangulation*. It refers to the combination of methodologies to fortify a study design.

Nontraditional or alternative forms of assessment

In terms of pedagogical points, the following nontraditional or alternative forms of assessment of classroom-based writing will be considered.

Rubrics

Rubrics are not a separate choice in assessment but they are day-to-day classroom assessment procedures. In order to create useful rubrics, the following points are important.

- Listing the purposes of the assessment instrument
- Describing the scale for students' performances
- Making criteria
- Considering revision

Portfolio assessment

A typical writing portfolio contains students' total writing output to show his/her general performance. It shows a student's work from the beginning of the term to the end, informing both the teacher and the student a chance to evaluate how much the latter's writing has improved. For portfolios to meet the goals of literacy assessment, they must be developed as follows:

- A wide range of notes and reflections are kept in the portfolio.
- Interaction between students and teachers is an integral part of portfolio assessment.
- Materials should be added to the portfolio by both teachers and students.
- Students are the owners of the portfolios.

Teachers can use portfolio for a variety of purposes, including:

- Making an intersection for instruction and assessment.
- Representing progress toward identified outcomes.

- Encouraging self-directed learning.
- Expanding the view of what is learned.
- Improving learning about learning.
- Giving opportunities for peer-supported growth.
- Providing a way for students to value themselves as learners.

Protocol analysis

It is known as thinking aloud activity. It is a description of the activities, ordered in time, in which a student engages while writing a task. It reveals the conscious processes involved in writing. In this approach, students are asked to record every thought that comes to mind during writing process. In order to enable students to protocol analysis, the teacher should serve as a model. It is suggested that composition contains three major processes: *planning*, *generating* the text based on the internal representation under the plan's guidance, and *editing* to examine the text for grammatical and semantic errors, and for failure to match the plan.

Learning log

Learning logs are a simple and clear way to help students integrate content, process, and personal feelings. Learning logs operate from students' learning from writing rather than writing what they have learned to have students make entries in their logs during the last five minutes of class. The message here is that short and frequent writing activity is more productive over time than infrequent and longer assignments. Learning logs are generally used in assessing literacy and become a vehicle for exchange among teachers and learners.

Journal entries

They are used as informal tools of assessment because they are personal and intimate. The teacher can write short notes in response to students' thought. Therefore, it can be an enjoyable activity which provides safety and freedom to be a writer. Journal entries are used primarily to give students an opportunity to express themselves on paper, feel confident that their ideas, observations, emotions, and writing will be accepted without criticism.

Dialogue journals

A dialogue journal is a written conversation in which a student and a teacher communicate regularly (daily, weekly, etc., depending on the educational setting) over a semester, school year, or course. Students write as much as they can and the teacher writes back regularly, responding to students' questions and comments, introducing new topics, or asking questions. The teacher is a participant in an ongoing, written conversation with the student, rather than an evaluator who corrects or comments on the student's writing. Dialogue journals help learners develop naturally an awareness of the communicative purpose of reading and writing as they participate in a written "conversations" with the teacher over an extended period of time.

Exam classes

Many English teachers sometimes tend to teach a class preparing for an exam such as IELTS and TOEFL. Even experienced teachers can find exam classes challenging to teach. Firstly, the stakes are higher. There is an obvious result for the students at the end and failure in the exam can be costly. As a teacher you should provide your students with the best chance of passing. Therefore, your impact in terms of motivation, organization and feedback on their performance can be conclusive. Secondly, you may find that the most effective approach to take and the type of activities you use is quite different from other classes you teach. Thirdly, you may find that you need more specific and detailed knowledge of the exams themselves and points and ideas for preparing students for success. Exam classes will be of particular interest to teachers who need to prepare students for Cambridge ESOL First Certificate and other exams in the Cambridge ESOL suite (PET, CAE, and Proficiency). It is suitable for recently qualified TEFL/TESOL teachers with an interest in improving in this area quickly and for more experienced teachers who find themselves teaching First Certificate classes and other exam classes for the first time.

An examination preparation course should include

- language work relevant to the need of the exam.
- tasks and activities to improve language awareness, ability ,and skills.
- specific practice on exam techniques e.g. multiple-choice questions, writing essays, reading comprehension, open cloze test, etc.
- working on study skills e.g. use of dictionaries and grammar books.

Current research findings

As nations search for ways to improve students' achievement, educators and policy makers continue to evaluate and reform their education systems. Educational testing, or assessment, is the main component of all education systems. Assessments can be used in schools to monitor educational systems for public accountability; help improve curricula; evaluate the effectiveness of teaching and instructional practices; measure students' achievement; and determine students' mastery of skills.

Conclusion

We have discussed the differences between test, evaluation, and measurement. There are many assessment and test models. The characteristics of good items such as item facility, item discrimination, and choice distribution and together as a whole such as practicality, reliability, validity, authenticity, washback, and interactiveness have been considered since the results of the test are important in decision making. The procedures of making a test have been mentioned. Test making is not an easy task. Therefore, it needs careful consideration. All language skills and components have particular assessment procedures. Cloze test and dictation have been examined thoroughly. Test scoring, feedback, principles for test-makers, principles for grading, grading on a curve, grading writing, grading speaking, alternative assessment, and exam classes are the other components of this chapter.

REFERENCES

Bagheri, M. S., Rahimi, F., & Riyasati, M. J. (2011). *A teacher   course moving beyond theory to practice.* Shiraz: Eideye Derakhshan

Burns, A., & Richards, J. C. (2012). *The Cambridge guide to   pedagogy and practice in second language teaching.* Cambridge: Cambridge University Press

Bartel, M. (July, 2009). *Encouraging creative thinking with awareness questions.* http://www.bartelart.com/arted/questions.html

Brown, J. D., & Bailey, K. M. (1984). A categorical instrument for   scoring second language writing skills. *Language learning,* 34, 21-42.

Brown, H. D. (2000). *Principles of language learning and teaching* (4th ed.), White Plains, NY: Pearson

Brown, H. D. (2001). *Teaching by principles: An interactive approach to language pedagogy* (2nd ed.), White Plains, NY: Pearson

Brown, H. D. & Abeywickrama, P. (2010). *Language assessment principles and classroom practices (2nd ed.).* White Plains, NY: Pearson Education

Burke, J. (1999). *The English teacher's companion.* Portsmouth, NH: Heinemann.

Cangelosi, S. J. (1988). *Classroom management strategies: Gaining and maintaining students' cooperation.* New York: Longman.

Celce-Murcia, M. (1991). *Teaching English as a second or foreign language.* (2nd ed.). New York: Newbury House.

Celce-Murcia, M., Brinton, D., & Goodwin, J. (1996). *Teaching pronunciation: Reference for teachers of English to speakers of other languages.* Cambridge: Cambridge University Press.

Chastain, K. (1998). *Developing second-language skills theory and practice (3rd ed.).* Harcourt Brace Jovanovich, Inc.

Clinton, B. L. (1992). Informative communication instruction: an application of theory and research to the elementary school classroom. *Communication education* (Annandale, VA), vol. 41, p. 54–67.

Dewey, J. (1933). *How we think: a restatement of the relation of reflective thinking to the educative process,* rev. ed.

Ellis, R. (2004). *Task-based language learning and teaching.* Oxford: Oxford university Press

Farhady, H., Jafarpur, A., & Birjandi, P. (1994). *Testing language skills: From theory to practice.* Tehran: SAMT.

Haller, E. et al.; Child, D.; Walberg, H. J. (1988). Can comprehension be taught: a quantitative synthesis. *Educational researcher* (Washington, DC), vol. 17, no. 9, p. 5–8.

Harmer, J. (2007). *How to Teach English* 2nd ed.) Essex: Longman.

Hughes, A. (2003). *Testing for language teachers* (2nd ed.). U.K: Cambridge University Press.

Hunt, A. & Beglar, D. (2005). A framework for developing EFL reading. *Reading in a Foreign Language, 17* (1) 23-59. Retrieved January 9, (2009). from

http://nflrc.hawaii.edu/rfl/Apri(2005)/hunt/hunt.pdf

Jensen, J. M. (1993). What do we know about the writing of elementary school children? *Language arts* (Urbana, IL), vol. 70, p. 290–94. 19

Kagan, S. (1994). *Cooperative learning.* San Clemente, CA: Kagan.

Kyriacou, Ch. (1991). *Essential teaching skills.* Oxford: Blackwell Education.

Kumaravadivelu, B. (1994). *The postmethod condition:* (E) merging strategies for second/foreign language teaching. TESOL Quarterly, 28, 27-48.

Kumaravadivelu, B. (2012). *Language teacher education for a global society: A modular model for knowing, analyzing, recognizing, doing, and seeing.* Routledge: New York & London

Larsen-Freeman, D. (2000). *Techniques and principles in language teaching (2nd ed.).*NY: Oxford University Press.

Tinoca, L., Son, S. H., & Williams, L. (Nov., 2001). *TIPS for teachers-asking good questions.* http://www.edb.utexas.edu/pbl/TIPS/question.html

Lyster, R., & Ranta, L. (1997). Corrective feedback and learner uptake: Negotiation of form in communicative classrooms. *Studies in second language acquisition*, 19, 37-66.

Munby, J. 1978. *Communicative syllabus design.* Cambridge: Cambridge University Press.

Nation, I.S.P., & Macalister. J. (2010). *Language curriculum design.* ESL & Applied Linguistics Professional Series. New York: Routledge.

Nunan, D. (1988). *Syllabus Design.* Oxford: Oxford University Press.

Nunan, D. (1989) *Designing tasks for the communicative classroom.* Cambridge: Cambridge University Press

Nunan, D. (1991) *Language Teaching Methodology*, Hemel Hempstead: Prentice Hall International.

Rashtchi, M., & Keyvanfar, A. **(1999)**. *ELT Quick'n'Easy.* Tehran: Rahnama Publications.

Richards, J. C., & Rodgers, T. S. (2001). *Approaches and methods in language teaching* (2nd ed.). Cambridge: Cambridge University Press.

Richards, J. C., & Renandya, W. A. (eds.) (2002). *Methodology in language teaching: an anthology of current practice.* Cambridge: Cambridge University Press.

Richards, J. C., Platt, J., & Platt, H. (2002). *Longman dictionary of teaching &*

applied linguistics(3ʳᵈ ed.). Essex: Longman.

Richterich, R. & Chancerel, J. L. (1977/80) *Identifying the needs of adults learning a foreign Language.* Oxford: Pergamon Press.

Rivers, W. (1981). *Teaching foreign language skills* (2ⁿᵈ ed.). Chicago: University of Chicago Press.

Scrivener, J. (1994). *Learning teaching.* Macmillian.

Guruprasad, P. R. (July 2009). Vol 6 No 7, the Gazette. *Applying Bloom's taxonomy to questioning techniques in the classroom.*

Ur, P. (1996). A *course in language teaching.* Cambridge: Cambridge University Press.

Walberg, H. J., & Fredrick, W.C. (1992). *Extending learning time.* Washington, DC: U.S. Department of Education, Office of Educational Research and Improvement.

Wallace, T., & Walberg, H.J. (1987). Personality traits and childhood environments of eminent essayists. *Gifted child quarterly* (Washington, DC), vols. 31, no. 2, p. 65–69.

Wang, C. M. (February 2003). Ideas on Teaching Volume 1, *Questioning techniques for active learning.* http://www.cdtl.nus.edu.sg/Ideas/iot2.htm

Willis, J. (1996). *A framework for task-based learning.* Essex: Longman.

Internet resources

http://www.englishclub.com
http://www.teachingenglishgames.com/Articles
http://www.teachingenglish.org.uk/knowledge-database
http://www.doe.in.gov/englishlanguagelearning
http://www.teachingcenter.wustl.edu/

www.ingramcontent.com/pod-product-compliance
Lightning Source LLC
Chambersburg PA
CBHW062101090426
42741CB00015B/3301